Revolutionary Education
Theory and Practice for Socialist Organizers

LIBERATION MEDIA

SAN FRANCISCO

Edited by
Nino Brown

Editorial Assistants
Hannah Dickinson, Mazda Majidi,
Gabriel Rockhill, and Marissa Sanchez

Staff
Jon Britton, Sarah Carlson, Anne Gamboni, Saul Kanowitz,
Susan Muysenburg, Keith Pavlik

Liberation Media
2969 Mission Street #201
San Francisco, CA 94110
(415) 821-6171
books@LiberationMedia.org
www.LiberationMedia.org

Revolutionary Education
Theory and Practice for Socialist Organizers

About Liberation School

Liberation School is an educational site for activists and fighters created by the Party for Socialism and Liberation. Maintained by a core editorial collective of PSL members, we are committed to providing political and historical clarity to the burning issues of our movement. The socialist digital school is for both PSL members and friends as well as all progressive and revolutionary activists.

In addition to in-depth articles, analysis, interviews and Party documents, Liberation School features a growing number of educational resources to help a new generation of revolutionaries learn, study and apply Marxist theory today.

Video and audio courses include "Black Struggle is Class Struggle," "Fascism and Global Class Struggle," "Comrade" and more. We also have study guides for classic texts by Engels, Marx, and Lenin, as well as for contemporary works like "Hammer and Hoe" and a number of PSL publications.

All materials can be found at LiberationSchool.org.

Revolutionary Education

Theory and Practice for Socialist Organizers

Introduction

Revolutionary education and the promotion of socialist consciousness

BY LIBERATION SCHOOL EDITORIAL COLLECTIVE

MARXIST theory is one of the most potent weapons the working and oppressed classes have. It is a weapon our class can and has used to not only win reforms but to build revolutionary societies where the people are in control, rather than profits. As the Party for Socialism and Liberation identified at our Third Party Congress in 2016, one of our primary tasks is to mend the "break in ideological continuity" that emerged after the overthrow of the Soviet Union. The communist movement will do so by establishing "the theory of revolutionary Marxism and the entire vision of workers' power" as a dominant guiding pole in people's struggles.[1]

Objective factors like rampant unemployment and the growing climate catastrophe have helped revive interest in socialism as the only alternative to the exploitation and oppression of capitalism and imperialism. While organizers cannot predict when a revolutionary opportunity will arise, we know that the objective conditions for such will present themselves as a result of capitalism's internal contradictions. In addition to building organizations that fight to improve people's lives in the here and now, one of our constant tasks as revolutionaries is to prepare the subjective factors for revolution. This means we have to organize our class, build connections to and relationships with communities and organizations, raise the political consciousness of the people and ourselves, and popularize socialism amongst ever wider groups. A socialist revolution will not take place spontaneously as a response to worsening conditions; it requires a mass revolutionary movement of millions of human beings who have the consciousness, confidence and desire to fight for it.

Education is a key component in preparing these subjective conditions for revolution. On a daily basis socialist and other progressive organizers and activists engage in educational processes. Here we define education broadly, for processes that take place both inside and outside of formal class settings. Organizers read the news, history and theory on our own and with each other, we organize and attend study and discussion groups, we attend and present at public forums, we write informational and agitational literature in response to the struggles we are engaged in, we converse with our neighbors and coworkers about politics and we even organize and teach classes and courses. The mentorship and training that every organizer both receives and offers to others, in the course of a struggle or campaign, all have educational dimensions to it. Active political education is crucial for revolutionary struggle because it raises the consciousness and long-term commitment of the people who will confront the deepening objective crises of capitalism.

Active political education is crucial for revolutionary struggle because it raises the consciousness and long-term commitment of the people who will confront the deepening objective crises of capitalism.

A good deal of revolutionary education involves explanation, argumentation, coming up with the appropriate formulation or slogan, recommending the right reading or the right speech, and generally promoting our analysis of the problems we face and the solutions to those problems. All of these educational activities are absolutely crucial, but they are only one aspect of education. Specifically, the activities listed above are about the political content of revolutionary education, what could be called the revolutionary curriculum.

The curriculum is about the political theories and goals we want to learn and teach. Pedagogy — the method and practice of teaching — on the other hand, is primarily about how we engage that curriculum. In other words, the curriculum refers to the "what" of education and pedagogy refers to the "how" of education, or to the different approaches we take to education, the kinds of attitudes we practice, the types of relationships we establish and how we understand our own teaching and learning and more.

Pedagogy is important because even the most appropriate, relevant and correct content can be engaged or taught in a way that turns people off, shuts them down or otherwise disengages them. Part of learning how to be a better organizer entails learning how to be a better educator. Without explicitly considering educational theory and practice, we will not have the frameworks, concepts and language to intentionally plan, revise, implement, reflect on, discuss and evaluate our educational practices. In this book, we focus on the pedagogy — and not the curriculum — of revolutionary education. The intent is not to tell you how to educate, but to provide you with resources to inform your own educational endeavors.

REVOLUTIONARY OPTIMISM
AND THE PRESUMPTION OF COMPETENCE

If you ask any teacher in any setting, they will tell you there is no "formula" or "recipe" for education. Corporate charter movements often try to produce such recipes — like Teach for America's "I do, you do, we do" rote learning method. But teaching is dependent on relationships, trust, respect and a host of other elements. All these can change day to day. Teaching on a Monday after a big fight broke out at a weekend party is different from teaching the next Wednesday when things have settled down a bit. Teaching in a pandemic is markedly different from teaching before one. These are just a few examples of the unpredictable forces that shape the educational experience.

Similarly, Marxist pedagogy is contingent on a multitude of factors: the dominant political ideology at the place and time (is it intensely anti-communist or more open?), the consciousness of students as individuals or as a collective (are they coming from a liberal issue-based organization or a strand of the movement?), the autonomy we are allowed in certain settings (is it an after-school club at a public/private school, a community meeting or a Party office?). And of course, there are other factors like different skills, personalities, time commitments, and relations between teachers and students.

There is a caricature of Marxism we might encounter in the movement and among left academics: the idea that Marxist revolution is predicated on the "enlightened" revolutionary teaching the "ignorant" masses. Nowhere do Marx or Engels even hint at this condescending notion, and neither do the revolutionaries following in their wake. As we will discuss in the first chapter, one of Lenin's main gripes with those "Marxists" who focused exclusively on bread-and-butter issues, what he called "trade-union consciousness," was their assumption that workers could only understand their immediate situation. It was also one of Marx and Engels' main critiques of the reformism of the Social Democratic Party in Germany. As Marx and (primarily or wholly) Engels wrote in an 1879 letter for internal circulation among some SDP leaders:

> For almost 40 years we have emphasized that the class struggle is the immediate motive force of history and, in particular, that the class struggle between bourgeoisie and proletariat is the great lever of modern social revolution; hence we cannot possibly co-operate with men who seek to eliminate that class struggle from the movement. At the founding of the International we expressly formulated the battle cry: The emancipation of the working class must be achieved by the working class itself. ... Hence we cannot cooperate with men who say openly that the workers are too uneducated to emancipate themselves, and must first be emancipated from above by philanthropic members of the upper and lower middle classes.[2]

What Marx and Engels are saying here is that we should always presume the competence of the working class. This does not mean we should presume the capitalist system sets everyone up for success. Quite the contrary: The system sets the masses up for poverty. What presuming competence does mean, however, is that we should assume by default that those we are organizing alongside have the capacity and potential for transforming their consciousness and ideas, habits and actions, political beliefs and commitments. We will not all have the same knowledge, but we always all have the same capacities for utilizing our intelligence.

Presuming competence also puts the responsibility on the educator, the revolutionary, the organizer and the organization, insofar as it means that if the student is not "getting it," then the problem lies with us. Too often educators displace our own incompetence onto students. This is not to say, as with "bad grades" in the classroom, that it is all the teacher's fault either. A Marxist approach to education requires looking beyond concepts such as the "innate" inability of the student and instead to a complex of factors, some of which are beyond and some of which are within our dominion. Our own teaching is one determining factor that is within our control.

OUTLINE OF THE BOOK

Because teaching is unpredictable and dynamic, we have to maintain flexibility with our educational tactics and strategies. The questions of what teaching strategies to use and when and how to use them, however, should be informed by Marxist pedagogical theories. This is why this book begins with several pieces on Marxist philosophies of education. The opening chapters are more theoretical and introduce some of the foundational educational theories in the Marxist tradition. While we give current examples of how they can inform our own practices today, they do not directly answer the question "What is to be done?" Instead, these theories provide different frameworks socialist organizers can use to refine our own teaching practices.

The book begins with chapters on educational practitioners and theorists who are more popularly known in the United States, but whose Marxist origins are often repressed or ignored. Chapter 1 focuses on Soviet psychologist Lev Vygotsky, who produced the first specifically historical-materialist theory of education. Vygotsky demonstrated that any person's or group's level of development and potential for future growth is not biologically fixed or socially predetermined. Instead, Vygotsky showed that people's development is dependent on their historical circumstances and based on social experiences. In other words, there is nothing essential in the student that explains why they have developed in a certain way or how they can develop in the future. Vygotsky developed his theory of the "Zone of Proximal Development" to help educators move students beyond their present level of development by guiding them through problem-solving scenarios. Many classroom teachers in the United States will have some familiarity with these concepts, while others may find them new and somewhat challenging. We believe the theory can be extended to the task of raising class consciousness among the working class, which requires meeting people where they are, accompanying through struggles and experiences that challenge their existing worldview, and then drawing out the lessons together.

The second chapter focuses on Paulo Freire's critique of oppressive education and the conception of revolutionary pedagogy he developed in response. Freire identified mainstream approaches to education as "banking pedagogy" in which students are seen as empty vessels to be filled with information by teachers. In this model, students are raw materials for the teacher to mold. Against this, Freire's pedagogy of the oppressed is based on shared dialogue and action in order to identify and then transform the social structures that must be transformed.

In Chapter 3, we build on Vygotsky's historical-materialist approach to intelligence and development to consider the kinds of attitudes teachers and students should embody to develop revolutionary consciousness. In particular, we look at research into how communities in struggle, in a sense, carry out Vygotsky's educational theory when more advanced community members help newer members develop their potential. We discuss the difference between having a "fixed" mindset and a "growth" mindset, and why the latter is so important for revolutionary organizers and for facilitating cadre development. It begins with a simple truth that we can never remind ourselves of too often: None of us were born comrades.

Although Marx never explicitly addressed pedagogy, Chapter 4 — the last theoretical chapter — examines the distinction Marx makes between the methods used for researching and for presenting. The method of research is an open-ended, messy and unpredictable process of studying and investigating a topic, whereas the method of presentation is a clear, linear and neat process of learning and understanding a topic. After discussing the distinction between learning and studying, we analyze how Marx navigated between both.

From here the book takes a more practical turn with concrete examples of Marxist pedagogy. In Chapter 5, we see the example of Guinea-Bissauan, anti-colonial revolutionary Amílcar Cabral, who offers an exceptional example of a revolutionary educator who takes Marxism as a dynamic theory rather than a fixed dogma. As a leader in the unified struggle against Portuguese colonialism in two of Portugal's African colonies, Guinea-Bissau and Cape Verde, Cabral exemplifies the revolutionary as educator, who wrote and theorized as he led. Cabral and his focus on revolutionary forms of education show us what inspired and deepened Freire's grasp of pedagogical praxis. They also demonstrate why Freire and Cabral's legacies continue to offer invaluable educational insights for communist organizers today.

In Chapter 6, we address the concepts of dual power and base building, which revolutionaries in the United States are wrestling with today. After clarifying what dual power is and providing historical and contemporary examples of it, we show — from the direct experience of our organization — how "serving the people" is a tactic for mobilizing the masses and building the party rather than as a political strategy in itself. Mutual aid, for example, is an educational tactic insofar as it teaches our communities who cares for their well-being, and who does not, and it helps build genuine relationships and create authentic dialogue with other working-class leaders and organizations.

In Chapter 7, we turn specifically to the issue of building cadre-based organizations through a mass-based approach. We address overcoming some of the educational obstacles to building revolutionary organizations, including the "paralysis of analysis," individualism and sectarianism.

A book on revolutionary pedagogy would not be complete without a chapter on militant journalism. Chapter 8 not only covers militant journalism, but it does so with Frank González, the director of Cuba's Prensa Latina news agency. González shows us a class-conscious approach to international journalism from the perspective of a socialist country. A view from Cuba into the "mentality" dominant in the United States completes the picture González paints. Such insights offer immense pedagogical lessons for progressive forces around the world and within the United States.

The final chapter is an interview with militant historian Sónia Vaz Borges. This provides an essential supplement to Chapter 5. As a child of Cape Verdean immigrants who grew up in Portugal, Vaz Borges provides indispensable insights into the so-called colonial mother country. The interview includes additional background on the movements leading up to the revolutionary struggle in Guinea-Bissau and Cape Verde.

The two appendices provide a range of tactics revolutionaries can deploy as they design and implement educational processes. The first appendix delineates different kinds of study and discussion questions you can use in your own educational programs and outreach. This is not meant as an instructional set of recipes to replicate. It is more of a general framework for thinking about how you might construct a set of reading and facilitation prompts to help you, your comrades and other educational participants. It will also help synthesize, apply and extend ideas in different directions based on your own local conditions.

The final appendix presents a series of tactics you can use for teaching or facilitating an educational meeting. We include an array of different tactics and delineate the particular purposes of each. While these are distinct tactics, you can — and should — feel free to combine them with each other and use them with the different kinds of questions articulated in the previous appendix.

We encourage readers to use this book as a tool to further the class struggle ideologically and practically. Marxist theory is the crystallization of the experience of the working class, its movements and political instruments, in struggle with a broad range of other trends and classes; it is never final or all inclusive, but open to future developments. The purpose of this book is to facilitate the training of growing numbers of revolutionary organizers and educators.

REVOLUTIONARY EDUCATION

The theories, examples, and components of revolutionary education explored in this book are intended to help socialist organizers as we work to popularize socialism and demonstrate to political theories and movements how socialism can address the pressing needs of working and oppressed people in the United States.

To win a socialist revolution in an imperialist country with a highly developed capitalist system like the United States, we must first win over large and significant segments of the population to socialism and to the belief that the masses here can lead a socialist transformation of society. This entails not only commitments to internationalism and the active solidarity with all national liberation struggles around the world, but also with all struggles of nationally oppressed peoples within this country. The latter have conclusively demonstrated that they are the sparks for a wide range of struggles and will play a vanguard role in the socialist revolution here.

Socialist consciousness will not grow on its own. It requires the organized and intentional efforts of an expansive base of militant organizers equipped to intervene in a variety of campaigns and movements. Such organizers are not only activists but also educators. They learn, study, reflect, teach, sum up and use the struggle as a school for developing themselves and thus the struggle itself. All of these actions are ways that we develop the subjective factor in building the revolutionary movement.

All revolutionary processes are inherently educational. From organizing meetings, forums and study groups to protest speeches, propaganda and agitation before the revolutionary moment, to the creation of new revolutionary educational and cultural institutions and the training of teachers and specialists after the seizure of power, revolution is pedagogical through and through. By focusing on the theory and practice of revolutionary education, we can accelerate the promotion of socialist consciousness and the creation of revolutionary organizations. □

Chapter 1

Vygotsky and the Marxist approach to education

BY CURRY MALOTT

O NE of the first specifically Marxist approaches to education emerged in the Soviet Union in the early 20th century and is credited to Lev Vygotsky. Vygotsky's name is now commonplace in the field of education worldwide. Most teachers can at least recall the name from their child development or educational psychology classes. His theories are still foundational but, as is the case with so many revolutionaries, they have been stripped of their Marxist foundations. One result is that the full revolutionary potential of Vygotsky's theories has remained largely unknown, not only inside schools and teacher education programs but also inside social movements.

This chapter introduces Vygotsky's theories on pedagogy and human development. It contextualizes them within the transition from Czarist Russia to the Soviet Union, draws out the main elements of his work that have utility for revolutionary organizers and provides concrete illustrations of their relevance today.

CONDITIONS IN CZARIST RUSSIA

Lev Semionovich Vygotsky was born in 1896 to a Jewish family in the town of Orsha, Belarus, at the time a part of the Russian Empire. Coming from such a family in Czarist Russia meant a lifetime of discrimination. Jewish people lived in restricted territories, were subject to strict quotas for university entrance and were excluded from certain occupations.

These restrictions nearly blocked Vygotsky's admittance to university despite his youthful brilliance. His experiences with anti-Jewish bigotry would go on to influence his later work in psychology.

Most clearly, these experiences pushed him to critique conceptions of the mind that treated the development of cognitive processes as purely internal to the individual, unaffected by the surrounding world.

Vygotsky's groundbreaking work was frequently and painfully interrupted by tuberculosis, which eventually killed him at the young age of 37. To his peers, he was a child genius. By the time he was 15 years old, he was known as the "little professor."

Vygotsky's contributions to educational psychology stemmed not only from his own research, but also from the impact of his environment: revolutionary Russia.

A COMMUNIST THEORY OF COGNITION

One central feature of Vygotsky's theory is the rejection of the "stagist" view of cognitive development. According to this view, all people, regardless of their social context or historical moment, develop according to predetermined and universal phases.[1] For example, the Swiss researcher, Jean Piaget, a contemporary of Vygotsky, developed a model of cognitive development based on four predetermined age-based stages that proceeded from basic sensory learning to complex, abstract thinking. Whatever utility this schema may have, Piaget's framework is rigid and ahistorical insofar as cognitive development evolves through fixed, natural, separate and unrelated stages.

Vygotsky demonstrated that cognitive development is not simply a matter of someone's biological makeup but is mediated by social factors. Consequently, as society changes, so too does the potential for cognitive development. Cognitive development is not about an individual's potential for development because individuals are always members of class and other social groups. Moreover, there's nothing "inside" or inherent in anyone that determines their path of intellectual growth.

Vygotsky's theories were deeply influenced and inspired by the Bolshevik Revolution, which coincided with Vygotsky's graduation from Moscow University in 1917. The Revolution transformed many disciplines and opened up new realms of inquiry and opportunities for young, formerly oppressed and marginalized scholars such as Vygotsky. The Bolshevik leadership heavily emphasized education after the revolution, to overturn the conservative, reactionary ideology that permeated the predominantly peasant, semi-feudalist society.

The cognitive development of peasants, in other words, was not the result of biology or their nationality, nor was it fixed forever; it was the result of human-created social conditions, it was historical, and could therefore be radically transformed. Lenin summed this up in his address to the First All-Russian Congress on Adult Education. He emphasized the working class and peasantry's thirst for knowledge, noting "how heavy the task of re-educating the masses was, the task of organization and instruction, spreading knowledge, combating that heritage of ignorance, primitiveness, barbarism and savagery that we took over."[2] As renowned Vygotskian scholar James Wertsch put it, "Vygotsky and his followers devoted every hour of their lives to making certain that the new socialist state, the first grand experiment based on Marxist-Leninist principles, would succeed."[3]

> The Bolshevik leadership heavily emphasized education after the revolution, to overturn the conservative, reactionary ideology that permeated the predominantly peasant, semi-feudalist society.

Vygotsky's work therefore was situated in one of the most intellectually and culturally stimulating settings of the 20th century. His project was dedicated to remaking psychology in Marxist terms in order to overcome the practical problems inherited from Czarist Russia, including illiteracy and the oppression of national minorities and women. Working in this exciting time of revolutionary transformation unleashed a radical desire for new knowledge. Vygotsky was taken by socialism's elevation of the general potential of cognitive development. By improving material conditions and celebrating and supporting — rather than attacking — the people's national diversity, new models of cognitive development could emerge.

Vygotsky worked out his core concepts in the field of child psychology, which he called the "Zone of Proximal Development (ZPD)."

Vygotsky showed that human beings' independent activity — what people can do on their own — is not the limit of what they can achieve with a teacher, peer or other leader. This is where the concept of the Zone of Proximal Development comes into play — defined by the distance between the existing level of development of a learner and their potential development

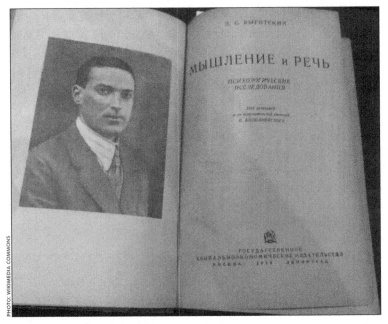

The original edition of Vygotsky's
'Thought and Language,' 1934

"through problem solving under adult guidance or in collaboration with more capable peers."[4] He demonstrated that by creating the spaces and practices for students to lead each other, and learn from each other, they can multiply their abilities and surpass preassigned expectations.

This concept is in some ways quite obvious to progressive people today who understand the universal value of education, reject the stultifying and excessively hierarchical forms of the bourgeois classroom, and reject the classification of individuals' potential based on class and racial hierarchies. But in the early 20th century, to reject those hierarchies and arbitrary limitations on students of all backgrounds was quite revolutionary and novel.

APPLYING VYGOTSKY'S INSIGHTS TO POLITICS TODAY

In what way do Vygotsky's core insights about learning remain important for all educators and organizers today? His concept of the Zone of Proximal Development has continued to be closely studied and hotly debated among educators; in the 1980s, his theories generated a whole school of pedagogy in the United States. But much of this discussion has occurred within the narrow parameters of teaching schools, erasing Vygotsky's corresponding political project: to fight a war on inequality, bigotry and poverty.

To take the Marxist educational approach outside of the formal classroom forces us to investigate the conditions determining the level of a person's or group's development. In the realm of political consciousness, furthermore, while all of us have been shaped by this racist, sexist, capitalist society, we never lose the ability to grow, change and think differently. Instead of writing people off, we should recognize that a) workers are influenced by the constant capitalist propaganda disseminated through the media and schooling, but b) can also be moved by progressive political education, the changing material conditions of life and most of all the class struggle.

For example, consider the rapid change in political consciousness ushered in the United States by the nationwide revolts against racism in the summer of 2020. The massive surge in consciousness was the product of the social conditions that brought people into the streets as well as the intervention of revolutionary organizers and activists. This movement both represented the emergence of a new radical consciousness, and in turn started to radicalize and move a broad mass of people on the issues of racial and class inequality. Regardless of where someone started when they decided to first join a protest, they were inevitably influenced by those around them — the speakers, the literature, the demands of the movement, the interactions with the state and with each other. The level of political development of the working class was starting to change rapidly. Almost overnight, it was no longer considered fringe or too radical to demand to abolish and defund the police. Socialist organizers then had to assess what people's potential level of development was, to advance new slogans, in order to most effectively carry out political education and build campaigns.

The 2020 uprising was an intense period, then, not just of class struggle — but also of political education. To extend the metaphor of Vygotsky's theory, the "students" (the working class engaged in anti-racist struggle) learned rapidly from each other and from their "peers" (more experienced organizers), absorbing new lessons quickly.

In the span of a few months, the working class as a whole skipped a few grades in a way that was considered inconceivable just before. The space of political possibility and openings in consciousness — or what could be called a "zone of proximal development" on a mass scale — increased dramatically in a way that was exhilarating and inspiring for all involved. It is useful to remember this during downturns in the struggle, when all might appear lost, when the working class seems largely inert and all the gains of the previous period are no longer so visible. That can radically change again, and it will.

What we need as organizers is an understanding of what we can do to maximize the potential for change to occur by identifying where the existing level of consciousness at every given moment is and how much and in what direction it can, with political intervention, change.

Correctly assessing where people are at — having a pulse of the people — is indispensable. Beyond having awareness of the larger political trends, this can be done with formal surveys and simply by asking people what they think. The more people that are talked to and the more outreach that is done, the better understanding organizers will have regarding a particular community's space to grow, what issues can be pushed on, what lessons can be drawn out.

Getting people to an educational event is only one step. Their presence alone does not ensure a successful breakthrough in consciousness. The movement's educational activities, like a good classroom, must create an inviting atmosphere and foster the willingness to engage (see Appendix B). If the event involves a political discussion around a short article, selecting and creating the most effective type of discussion questions for the audience and their particular level of development is key (see Appendix A). The questions should be within the same type of range that we outlined above — in the space between what people already know and experience on their own and what their consciousness can be moved to next with some discussion and guidance. This is the essence of good organizing and educating, not throwing out the most advanced concepts and questions at any given point. Offering participants a way to make connections to their own experiences tends to be an effective way to foster the willingness needed to advance political development.

The other factor Vygotsky identified in child psychology as necessary for growth is play or imagination. That is, people need to be able to think of themselves and the world as different than it is. Here too, Marxist organizers must be creative. Appendix B offers many activity ideas, such as role plays, that can help people achieve their potential political development. Of course as Marxists our goal is not just learning for the sake of learning, but for building a mass movement, winning necessary reforms, and ultimately, state power.

Vygotsky further defined the zone of proximal development as "those functions that have not yet matured but are in the process of maturation, functions that can mature tomorrow but are currently in an embryonic state. These functions could be termed the "buds" or "flowers" of development rather than the "fruits" of development.[5]

Vygotsky referred to potential developmental levels as "buds" or "flowers" rather than "fruits" because they are in the process of coming into being and therefore not yet fully ripe. Further, their process of coming into being is not predetermined. No one can know in advance what form the developed function will take. This is the same open-minded but optimistic outlook that organizers must take to the political consciousness of the working class — always reaching for and emphasizing that which is budding and could flower, and ultimately bear fruit. □

Chapter 2

Pedagogy of the oppressed for revolution

Paulo Freire and revolutionary leadership

BY DEREK R. FORD

PAULO Freire's "Pedagogy of the Oppressed" is a classic among progressive educators, organizers and revolutionaries. Although it is sometimes taken as a "how to" instructional book, it is really a theoretical reflection on Freire's own experiences teaching peasants how to read and write, a theory he extends to revolutionary movements, leadership and organization.

After spending 70 days in prison for the "treachery" of teaching poor peasants to read and write, he was exiled from his native Brazil following a military junta taking power in 1964. He eventually settled in Chile until 1969, where he wrote "Pedagogy of the Oppressed." The book has been targeted by the U.S. right wing and is currently banned from public schools in Arizona. It addresses the educational components of revolutionary movements and, as such, is littered with references to Marx, Lenin, Guevara and others. Specifically, the book is concerned with how the revolutionary leadership pushes the struggle forward, how it teaches and learns from the mass movement.

THE PEDAGOGIES OF OPPRESSION AND LIBERATION

The pedagogy of the oppressed has two stages. During the first stage, "the oppressed unveil the world of oppression and through praxis commit themselves to its transformation." During the second stage, which is after the world of oppression has been transformed, "this pedagogy ceases to belong to the oppressed and becomes a pedagogy of all people in the process of permanent liberation."[1]

The first stage of Freire's pedagogy addresses how the oppressed view and relate to the world. It begins by acknowledging that the oppressed possess both an oppressed consciousness and an oppressor consciousness. The oppressor consciousness is the enemy that needs to be liquidated: "The oppressor consciousness tends to transform everything surrounding it into an object of its domination. The earth, property, production, the creations of people, people themselves, time — everything is reduced to the status of objects at its disposal."[2]

This is what capitalism does: It takes everything and makes it into private property, including our ability to labor. This has a profound impact on the world, even instilling the oppressor consciousness in the oppressed. Thus, we have to distinguish an oppressor consciousness from the oppressed person, and we have to transform that consciousness to liberate the person.

The way that we engage in that transformation is crucial, and this is where the question of pedagogy comes into play. The traditional form of pedagogy Freire calls "banking pedagogy." In banking pedagogy, the teacher is the one who possesses knowledge and the students are empty containers into which the teacher must deposit their knowledge (like depositing money in a bank). The more the teacher fills the receptacle, the better teacher they are. The content remains abstract to the student, disconnected from the world and external to the student's life. Banking pedagogy — which is what most of us in the United States have experienced in public schools — assumes that the oppressed are ignorant and naïve. Further, it treats the oppressed as objects in the same way that capitalism does. Students are objects that the teacher works on. For Freire, education must be rooted in the daily lives and experiences of students, who are subjects rather than objects.

The correct educational method for revolutionaries is dialogue, which means something very specific. To truly engage in dialogue means becoming partners with the people. In this situation, "the teacher is no longer merely the-one-who-teaches, but one who is himself taught in dialogue with the students, who in turn while being taught also teaches. They become jointly responsible for a process in which all grow."[3] This process is referred to in Portuguese as conscientização, or coming-to-critical-consciousness.

A decisive element in the location and direction of conscientização is the pedagogical relationship. This relates to Freire's critique of the banking model of education and to his reconception of the

Mural in the Faculty of Education and Humanities,
University del Bío-Bío in Concepción, Chile

teacher-student relationship. The dialogic model, unlike the banking model, is a relationship between teacher and student that is more — but, and this is crucial, not completely — horizontal. In this schema, "people teach each other, mediated by the world, by the cognizable objects which in banking education are 'owned' by the teacher."[4] The teacher does not relinquish authority or power, as if that was even possible. Instead, the teacher takes responsibility for producing new critical knowledge of reality with the student.

PEDAGOGY CANNOT REPLACE POLITICS

While the pedagogical relationship and process are important parts of Freire's thought, they have tended to be isolated from Freire's ideological commitments and have come to stand in for Freire's entire work. As a graduate student in a fairly critical school of education, I was only assigned the first two chapters of his book, and I am convinced this is common practice. These chapters are rich: They are where he denounces banking pedagogy and formulates dialogical pedagogy in response. Yet we stop reading before we discover the reason he bothered writing the book in the first place.

By selectively reading the book, Freire's dialogic pedagogy is substituted wholesale for his broader conceptual and political work, his vocabularies and theories that generated new understandings of education and revolution. There is nothing inherent in dialogue or dialogic pedagogy that necessarily leads to progressive, critical understandings.

For this to happen, the content must be placed in a particular context by a teacher. Peter McLaren is one of the few U.S. educational theorists to insist on Freire's revolutionary commitments (and a student and comrade of Freire himself). McLaren goes so far as to say that "political choices and ideological paths chosen by teachers are the fundamental stuff of Freirean pedagogy."[5] We cannot divorce the methodology from the ideology, the theory from the method, or the critical from the pedagogy in Freire's work.

THE DANGEROUS FOURTH CHAPTER

Freire begins the last chapter of "Pedagogy of the Oppressed" with "Lenin's famous statement: 'Without revolutionary theory there can be no revolutionary movement,'" which Freire rephrases. Freire insists that revolutions are achieved neither by verbalism nor by activism "but rather with praxis, that is, with reflection and action directed at the structures to be transformed."[6] It would be just as wrong to claim that reflecting on and helping name oppression to the people is enough for revolution as to claim that activism is enough for revolution.

The task for revolutionaries is to engage with our class and our people in true, authentic dialogue, reflection and action. If we have dialogue and reflection without action, then we are little more than armchair revolutionaries. On the other hand, if we have only action without dialogue and reflection, we are mere activists and remain incapable of leading a revolution and erecting a new society.

Reflection and action are not divisions of labor between revolutionary leaders and the people, whereby the leaders think and direct and the people are only able to act on the leaders' orders. "Revolutionary leaders," he writes, "do bear the responsibility for coordination and, at times, direction — but leaders who deny praxis to the oppressed thereby invalidate their own praxis."[7] People and revolutionary leaders act together, building and acting in unity before, during and after the revolution.

The prerequisite for such leadership is the rejection of the "myth of the ignorance of the people."[8] Freire acknowledges that revolutionary leaders, "due to their revolutionary consciousness," have "a level of revolutionary knowledge different from the level of empirical knowledge held by the people."[9] The act of dialogue unites lived experience with revolutionary theory so people understand what causes their lived experience to be as it is. This is a restatement of Lenin's conviction that spontaneous knowledge of exploitation and oppression must be transformed through the party into revolutionary consciousness of the relationship of our experience to the relationship of broader social, economic and political forces at differing scales: within the factory, the city, the state and the world.

This is a Marxist philosophy of education in that, as we covered in the introduction, it rests on the presumption of competence. We can see this at work in "What is to be Done?" as Lenin argues against economist Marxists, who hold that the working class develops its own political consciousness spontaneously as a result of daily struggles with the bosses. Lenin argued that spontaneity was only consciousness "in an embryonic form," and that something more was needed. Spontaneity is necessary but is ultimately limited to "what is 'at the present time.'"[10] In other words, spontaneity by itself is not able to look beyond isolated daily struggles and forward to a new society. Lenin called the spontaneously generated mindset "trade-union consciousness."

Lenin believed workers were capable of more than trade-union consciousness. He actually derided those who insisted on appealing to the "average worker": "You gentlemen, who are so much concerned about the 'average worker,' as a matter of fact, rather insult the workers by your desire to talk down to them when discussing labor politics and labor organization." He wrote that organizers had actually held workers "back by our silly speeches about what 'can be understood' by the masses of the workers."[11] The economist organizers treated workers as objects rather than subjects. They did not believe in the people or their potential.

When Freire argues that revolutionary leadership should be open to and trusting of the people, he calls on Lenin. "As Lenin pointed out," he writes, "the more a revolution requires theory, the more its leaders must be with the people in order to stand against the power of oppression."[12] This is not a naïve acquiesce but a belief in the power of the masses to become not only agents of revolutionary movements but creators of revolutionary theory through the party.

As Lenin also observed, the party creates a particular group of theoreticians. In reference to the party Lenin writes, "all distinctions as between workers and intellectuals ... must be obliterated."[13]

There is no abstract celebration of "horizontalism" within such a pedagogy. The form of the revolution and its leadership are not predetermined or abstractly posited; it can be more horizontal or more vertical and triangular, depending on the circumstances. Here, Freire turns to Fidel Castro and the Cuban Revolution to argue that their historical conditions compelled them to revolt without building widely with the people. Yet the leadership pursued this task immediately after taking power through organization, specifically the party. Tyson Lewis is one of the few to observe that "Freire himself clearly saw his pedagogy as a tool to be used within revolutionary organization to mediate the various relationships between the oppressed and the leaders of resistance."[14] As this book will show in Chapter 5, this is why Freire looked so favorably upon Amílcar Cabral.

UNITING POLITICS AND PEDAGOGY FOR THE OPPRESSED

Revolutionary organizers, therefore, are defined not just by the revolutionary ideals they hold or actions they take, but by their humility, patience and willingness to engage with all exploited and oppressed people. It is not possible for us to "implant" the conviction to fight and struggle in others. Coming-to-critical-consciousness is a delicate and contingent process that cannot be scripted in advance. Still, there are a few general components to it.

First, we have to truly get to know our people, their problems and their aspirations. This means that we have to learn from people, acknowledging that, even if this is their first demonstration, or even if they voted for a Democrat in the last election, they have something to teach us. The more experiences we learn from the people the richer our theories are and the more connection they can have to the daily realities of workers and oppressed people today. Our class is bursting with creative and intellectual powers that capitalist society does not allow us to express or develop. The revolutionary party is stronger the more it cultivates these powers.

Second, we have to provide opportunities for others to understand their problems in a deeper and wider context, and to push their aspirations forward. Freire gives a concrete and relatable example:

... if at a given historical moment the basic aspiration of the people goes no further than a demand for salary increases, the leaders can commit one of two errors. They can limit their action to stimulating this one demand or they can overrule this popular aspiration and substitute something more far-reaching — but something which has not yet come to the forefront of the people's attention. ... The solution lies in synthesis: The leaders must on the one hand identify with the people's demand for higher salaries, while on the other they must pose the meaning of that very demand as a problem. By doing this, the leaders pose as a problem a real, concrete, historical situation of which the salary demand is one dimension. It will thereby become clear that salary demands alone cannot comprise a definitive solution.[15]

Through this process, both the people and the revolutionary leadership act together and collectively name the world. Genuine knowledge is produced, authentic action is taken and real conviction for the struggle is strengthened.

Freire's popularity presents an opening to draw many into the struggle and, in particular, the communist movement. By reestablishing the link between his pedagogy and politics, we can draw those who admire his work into the movement. At the same time, we can better understand, adapt and practice his pedagogical principles in our day-to-day organizing. "Only in the encounter of the people with the revolutionary leaders," Freire writes in the book's last sentence, "can this [revolutionary] theory be built."[16] □

Chapter 3

Comrades: Made, not born

BY JANE CUTTER

ALL revolutionary politics are predicated on revolutionary optimism: the belief, rooted in experiences in the struggle, that workers and the oppressed can and will win. Yet revolutionary optimism does not just apply to the masses as a whole. Revolutionary organizers believe not just in the potential of the masses, but of individuals as well.

Recently popularized research on "mindset" and learning may shed additional light on this topic. It may help activists and organizers, not only with their own development, but in developing the potential of others with whom they come into contact. Before delving into what "mindset" is and how understanding it could be of interest to organizers, it would be useful to review a Marxist understanding of "intelligence" in contrast with bourgeois and racist conceptions.

Most people would probably agree that "being smart" is a desirable attribute. The nature of "intelligence" or "intelligences" is beyond the scope of this article. But the discourse over intelligence seems to break down into two broad narratives: intelligence as an innate characteristic of individuals versus intelligence as socially defined and constructed behaviors and habits of mind.

Is one born with a set amount of intelligence, or can intelligence change and grow over the course of a lifetime? The notion that people are born with a fixed level of intelligence is one that has been picked up by racist elements in society who have used spurious "science" to make a case for the alleged superiority of white people. If intelligence is not simply a fixed attribute of individuals, how is it (or other forms of competence) socially constructed and determined? And what is the role of the individual in fostering the growth of one's own practice of competence?

PSL 10th anniversary conference in Los Angeles

To broadly summarize a socialist approach to "intelligence," one might say: Not only is "intelligence" a dynamic characteristic that can change over the course of an individual's life, but, moreover, what counts as intelligence also changes in response to changes in the structure of human society, including developments in the means of production. For instance, during the Middle Ages, the ability to hand-copy documents was viewed as the sign of a true intellectual. But the invention of the printing press and now, photocopiers and printers, have made hand-copying mostly irrelevant.

Dominant conceptions of intelligence usually serve to reinforce capitalism and its various forms of oppression, from racism to ableism. Any socialist approach to intelligence must take this into account, interrogating how certain standards of intelligence do this and keeping our definition open to its various manifestations.

VYGOTSKY AND THE ZONE OF PROXIMAL DEVELOPMENT

As we previously wrote, Vygotsky's work is foundational to our understanding of this question. In the context of the early days of the Russian Revolution, Vygotsky was a pioneer of communist psychology who introduced the sociocultural or sociohistorical analysis of human development. Vygotskian analysis sees human development as a synthesis of biological, social and historical factors. Each child develops in the context of a particular group structure located in a particular culture at a particular time in history. Each of these factors interacts to influence the child's physical, mental and emotional development. In turn, what counts as development in the first place is also the product of historical and material conditions.

Vygotsky is best known today in the West for his theory of the Zone of Proximal Development. Again, this is the idea that learning occurs when someone aids the learner in doing that which they cannot yet do independently. Instead of seeing intelligence as a static attribute, Vygotsky was interested in the child's ZPD. Rather than looking at how much a child had already learned as a means of assessing intelligence, Vygotsky was more interested in what the child could potentially do. He also took into consideration the understanding that what one has the potential to learn is also itself socially and historically conditioned.

COMMUNITIES OF PRACTICE AND MINDSET

In more recent years, ethnographers and educators have explored the concept of communities of practice as a site for the development of the ZPD. Researchers have looked at tailors, Alcoholics Anonymous, party members, teachers and others as forming communities of practice where more experienced community members help newer community members develop competence in the ways of the community. Again, this concept has clear relevance to the movement, where we can conceptualize political organizations as communities of practice in which the potential of new activists to do various things is developed through interaction with more experienced members — from writing, public speaking, project management and community outreach to logistics, security, street tactics and broader bodies of knowledge like studying and applying theory.

Carol Dweck's concept of mindset recently became quite popular. Her seminal research looked at children who were given a relatively easy puzzle to solve.[1] One group was praised for their efforts and the other group was praised for being smart. The children were then given another, more difficult puzzle to solve. Those praised for effort persevered and solved the harder puzzle. Those praised for intelligence tended to give up in the face of a more challenging task.

Ultimately, Dweck identified something that she termed "mindset" as the key to developing potential. Learners with a "growth" mindset tend to believe that academic success is a product of effort, even when the learning task is difficult, while those with a "set" or "fixed" mindset tend to believe that success is a result of innate ability. A growth mindset has been correlated with greater academic success as compared to a fixed mindset. Angela Duckworth's related concept of "grit" (perseverance in the face of difficulty plus passion) as well as Steele's stereotype threat (lowered performance when test conditions evoke knowledge of a stereotype of the participant's identity group — a variant on "set" or fixed mindset) have also become widely known among educators.[2]

THE MISUSE OF GROWTH MINDSET AND 'GRIT'

Given that learning and "intelligence" are socially constructed between the learner, the teacher and the sociocultural context, concepts of mindset, grit and other elements of learner agency must be understood as contextual, not as determining factors existing independently or solely as attributes of individuals.

In the context of contemporary neoliberal education reform, mindset and grit have been misused, especially in racist ways.[3] Instead of fighting the gross inequalities in the education system — by reducing class sizes, placing adequate support staff in every school, guaranteeing housing, food and health care for children, as well as implementing culturally appropriate and anti-racist curricula — teachers are taught to praise children differently and to positively reinforce effort and "grit." While there is no harm in reinforcing effort, the new focus on grit and mindset smacks of the "pull yourself up by your bootstraps" ideology, divorced from efforts to tackle the inherently inequitable social conditions in which children are learning today. Even Duckworth, the scholar behind the concept of "grit," has criticized the uses to which her concept has been put.[4]

It is immoral to tell hungry, homeless children or those traumatized by police brutality to be more "gritty," when in fact the most oppressed already put in tremendous effort just to survive. Further, because of how intelligence is defined by the U.S. schooling system, the vast knowledge and skills of children from oppressed communities are totally disregarded.

ORGANIZING AND GROWTH MINDSET

That said, is there a place for growth mindset among communists? I would argue yes, there is.

In the recent uptick of interest in socialism, I have seen the utility of a growth mindset among so many new activists. As an organizer, I have met people whom I frankly doubted had the capacity to become good comrades based on how they presented when we first met. Despite what I saw as unpromising attributes and prior experiences, some individuals were willing to participate, take on new tasks, accept criticism, and keep trying. Beyond learning communist theory and history, these activists became real organizers by developing skills and habits of mind such as discipline, self-sacrifice, humility, investigation, compassionate listening and more.

> *All progressive people must be willing to go beyond our comfort zones, learn from experiences, work collaboratively, accept discipline and make sacrifices.*

I have also met those who say they want to be organizers but express ideas more reflective of a fixed mindset. When challenged to make changes, these fixed-mindset people say something like: "People who can make that change are different, or special, smarter or stronger than me," or "I'm not like that so I can't do it." This becomes an excuse to not change behavior or try new or difficult things. When fixed-minded socialists experience a challenge or failure, they become discouraged and want to give up instead of trying to figure out how to learn from the experience.

All progressive people must be willing to go beyond our comfort zones, learn from experiences, work collaboratively, accept discipline and make sacrifices. As organizers we must also believe this about potential recruits. We cannot write off anyone with a desire to struggle based on their present level of development. Instead, we must have revolutionary optimism about the potential for further development. □

Chapter 4

Marx's pedagogies then and now

Research and presentation

BY DEREK R. FORD

A **FTER** surveying the educational theories and practices of revolutionaries and educators in the Marxist tradition, in this chapter we look at Marx's own pedagogical practice. Although Marx considered education at various points, he did not write about pedagogy. He did, however, make an important remark that is pedagogical in nature in the afterword to the second German edition of the first volume of "Capital." Here Marx distinguished the process of research (Forschung) from the method of presentation (Darstellung). This short but sharp passage is important for those who are taking up their own self-study of Marx's texts — which at times can be quite challenging — and generally for organizers as we take on tasks related to research and presentation in our own movements today.

In the section, Marx is responding to an assessment of "Capital," that had appeared in the European Messenger magazine based in St. Petersburg. The article focused on Marx's method of presentation and commended Marx for showing the laws of capitalism and of social transformation. Marx briefly noted the necessary differences between inquiry and presentation, differences that are pedagogical. Marx writes:

> Of course the method of presentation must differ in form from that of inquiry. The latter has to appropriate the material in detail, to analyze its different forms of development, to trace out their inner connection. Only after this work is done, can the actual movement be adequately described. If this is done successfully, if the life of the subject-matter is ideally reflected as in a mirror, then it may appear as if we had before us a mere a priori [or self-evident] construction.[1]

I think that Marx is describing two different pedagogies — or educational processes — here. The first, the method of inquiry or research, is one that examines material in all of its nuances and relationships, tracing out the different lineages, past, present and future potential forms of development, and how they relate to each other, and more. Researching is a process that entails wandering around, looking for connections, thinking you are onto something and then following it to a dead end, generating ideas, getting lost in the archives (whether they be in a library or on the internet) and so on. The questions are limitless and the possibilities are endless.

When researching, you have a goal in mind but the goal does not totally dictate everything you do. Marx researched to understand the inner logics and dynamics of capital, how these came to be, what impact they had and might have on the world and how the contradictions can be seized during the class struggle. But this goal was not always at the forefront of his mind. What we might read as "digressions" in his work are often the reality that the end goal had to be suspended at moments for research to continue. In fact, a lot of what we consider "distraction" or "procrastination" in schooling might actually be profound moments of research.

Research, however, cannot last forever, especially for revolutionaries. The goal is not just to understand the world, but to change it — and that requires a clear presentation of one's position. Presentation takes a totally different pedagogical form. It begins with a predetermined end that guides the demonstration from the start to the end. It begins with the most elementary building blocks and proceeds linearly toward the end goal. Whereas researching is about means, presentation is about ends: The ends structure everything that comes before.

Marx's "Capital" is a presentation of a very particular type. It leaves the historical beginnings of capitalism and leaves it to the very end of Volume 1. Here we learn that it was through slavery, colonialism, legal and extralegal theft, individual and state violence, and repression, that capitalism came to be. But he does not begin here because he is not attempting to tell the history of capitalism; rather he wants to convey the inner logic of capitalism and its intrinsic contradictions as it was most fully developed in England, and in some ways working from the inside out.

POLITICS AND EXAMPLES OF MARX'S PEDAGOGIES

Both presentation and research are of course necessary and Marx did a great deal of both. Even though Marx never wrote about pedagogy, his body of work provides us with potent examples of how he put them into practice. Two works in particular illuminate Marx's pedagogies in action: the "Grundrisse: Foundations of the Critique of Political Economy" (rough draft) and Volume 1 of "Capital."

The "Grundrisse" consists of a series of notes written in the frantic days of 1857-1858 and is a collection of eight notebooks. They were effectively lost for decades until they were discovered and then first published in 1939 in the Soviet Union and made available in Europe and the United States during the 1960s and 70s. Never intended for publication, they are a series of research notes, or traces of Marx's studying, which Eric Hobsbawm says, were "written in a sort of private intellectual shorthand which is sometimes impenetrable, in the form of rough notes interspersed with asides which, however clear they may have been to Marx, are often ambiguous to us." As a result, "anyone who has tried to translate the manuscript or even to study and interpret it, will know that it is sometimes quite impossible to put the meaning of some sibylline passage beyond all reasonable doubt."[2]

The "Grundrisse" notebooks are quite different from the first volume of "Capital," Marx's real magnum opus, the only volume published (and translated and republished) during Marx's lifetime. The "Grundrisse" is almost pure research (because they were notes Marx was not trying to present to others), while "Capital" is almost pure presentation (because it was meant to articulate the inner workings of capital to others).

For two distinct positions on these works, consider Louis Althusser and Antonio Negri. The former wrote that "Capital" is the only book "by which Marx has to be judged."[3] It was the "mature" Marx, clearly broken from his Hegelian roots (which still inflect the "Grundrisse") and any mention of humanism. Althusser, a lifelong member of the French Communist Party, was intervening in debates over "humanism" that he saw as diluting or abandoning the class struggle. Instead of proletarians versus the bourgeoisie, the colonizers versus the colonized, it was "humans"; a non-class category bereft of an enemy against which to struggle. Althusser returned to "Capital" to combat this trend.

The Cuban Literacy Brigades exemplify Marxist pedagogies as they play out inside and outside of classrooms.

On the other side, Antonio Negri contrasted the "Grundrisse" with "Capital" in a more favorable light because of its "incredible openness." "Capital," according to Negri, was a closed, determinate and objective book where contradictions resolved themselves. Negri did not dismiss "Capital," of course, but insisted that the book only represented one aspect of Marxism. The "Grundrisse" was an endless unfolding of research and, for Negri, openness and possibility. "Capital," on the contrary, was more limited precisely because of its "categorical presentation."[4] In essence, the "Grundrisse" was more open because it is a series of notebooks in which Marx discovers something and presents it, which brings forth a new problem, which then opens up a new field of inquiry, and so on.

Most Marxists agree that "Capital" represents Marx's highest work of thought precisely because the presentation was so elegant, clear, and compelling. "Capital" is guided by a pedagogy of presentation that begins with something simple and obvious (the commodity), and then goes deeper and deeper until we see that this "trivial" appearing thing that is all around us is an active crystallization of a series of ongoing struggles, like those between and within classes and the state that play out differently over history, that assume different forms (like technology and machinery), and so on.

RESEARCH AND PRESENTATION IN 'CAPITAL' AND THE 'GRUNDRISSE'

Marx's distinction between research/presentation is not hard and fast; it is not even as firmly delineated as Althusser and Negri insisted. Marx sought to understand, articulate, learn, and relay the precise logics of capital, its contradictions, and how the working class has seized and can seize on these contradictions to institute the revolutionary transition to communism. At the same time, he knew he could not complete this project because no one can fully delineate all the processes of capitalism so long as it exists, as capital is by definition a dynamic social relation, always in motion and in the process of change. This is one aspect of capital that Marx and Engels marveled at in the "Manifesto of the Communist Party":

> The bourgeoisie cannot exist without constantly revolutionizing the instruments of production, and thereby the relations of production, and with them the whole relations of society. Conservation of the old modes of production in unaltered form, was, on the contrary, the first condition of existence for all earlier industrial classes. Constant revolutionizing of production, uninterrupted disturbance of all social conditions, everlasting uncertainty and agitation distinguish the bourgeois epoch from all earlier ones. All fixed, fast-frozen relations, with their train of ancient and venerable prejudices and opinions, are swept away, all new-formed ones become antiquated before they can ossify. All that is solid melts into air, all that is holy is profaned, and man is at last compelled to face with sober senses his real conditions of life, and his relations with his kind.[5]

Indeed, when one reads the various outlines that Marx presented for "Capital" in the "Grundrisse" and elsewhere, it is clear that he was taking on a project he knew he could never finish. He wanted to write volumes on the state, the world market, foreign trade, wages, the history of theory and more. Even in the first volume of "Capital," we see traces of Marx's never-ending studying in the various places he notes an absolutely crucial point — one we "must understand" — only to move on by acknowledging he cannot address it here and it will have to wait until later: until he has studied some more. Sometimes, like when he brings up credit and rent in Volume 1, he does return to them in Volume 3. But other times he never does; he never found the time for more research.

The writings of Marx, Engels and other Marxists still explain the workings of capitalism today because they get at its fundamental dynamics and contradictions, even if they take on different weight at different moments. And even though Marx could not — and never claimed to — predict how capital would develop after his death, these dynamics and contradictions remained fundamental cornerstones for subsequent revolutionaries to take up, who extended his critique and method to prepare the groundwork for revolutionary action in their own era. Marxism develops by returning to the process of research and studying, to inquiry, to tracing new lineages, and discovering what Marx as an individual did not or could not write about.

> *The writings of Marx, Engels and other Marxists still explain the workings of capitalism today because they get at its fundamental dynamics and contradictions, even if they take on different weight at different moments.*

Marx's own turns between inquiry and presentation were dictated not only by his health problems but by the ups and downs of the market as well as the workers' movement. After the failure of the 1848 bourgeois-democratic revolutions, at which point Marx was exiled to England, he did not see the prospect of another revolutionary situation on the horizon. Absent a new revolutionary situation, Marx began his study of political economy in earnest. With the capitalist crisis of the mid 1850s, he was forced to speed up his research. When the Paris Commune erupted on March 18, 1871, he left his work on "Capital" to write about that. After the first volume of "Capital" was published, the other two major works he wrote before he died were "The Civil War in France" (1871) on the Paris Commune and the "Critique of the Gotha Programme" (1875) — which was not published until after Marx's death but that circulated widely amongst the newly-formed Social Democratic Party. Marx even pushed the publication of the second volume of "Capital" back because he was waiting to see how the European and U.S. economic crisis of 1873 would turn out.

RESEARCH AND PRESENTATION IN 'CAPITAL'

Both the "Grundrisse" and "Capital" represent different ways Marx engaged learning and studying. Consider, for example, the chapter in "Capital" on what established the "normal" workday, where Marx announces that "between equal rights force decides."[6] Here he means that between the established "rights" of the capitalists to set the terms of work for the employees, and the "rights" of the workers to decide on what terms they will be contracted for work, there is no magic number set by the market. It depends on the relative strength of the two classes, and their organizations, in their struggle against one another. Up until this point, Marx had taken bourgeois political theory at face value, but here the reality of the struggle forces a leap so that he must depart from abstracted mathematical formulas to the living struggle. The chapter presents a narrative of the struggle in England throughout the 19th century, one that is filled with contradictory alliances and betrayals, advances and defeats. It is a struggle waged not by individuals but by collectives: capitalists and workers together through the mediation of the state. Moreover, in a footnote he acknowledges the role that Protestant ideology played in the process "by changing almost all the traditional holidays into workdays" and later the role of the anti-slavery struggle in the United States.[7] There is nothing predictable or deterministic about any of this; and this is what we affirm when we say that class struggle is the motor of history and the motor of revolutionary transformation.

Another example of the importance of research and inquiry within the largely linear presentation of "Capital" is the very last two chapters.

In the penultimate chapter, Marx presented a clear and concise dialectical and historical materialist analysis of the tendency of capitalist accumulation, and how the contradictions of capitalism might result in particular revolutionary paths.

Marx begins Chapter 32 with the scattered private property of individuals in petty manufacture, handicraft and peasant labor. These methods prevented the concentration of means of production, preserving a more rudimentary division of labor. This in turn limited the cooperation of labor (social labor), and obstructed the formation of the collective laborer.

Marx referred to the working day as a struggle waged not by individuals but by collectives. Here, an eight-hour day march in Melbourne, Australia, circa 1900

Halfway through this first paragraph, Marx notes that "at a certain stage of development," these property relations created "the material agencies for its own dissolution," producing "new passions" that "the old social organization" prevented.[8] Individual private property was annihilated by capital and, through theft, colonialism and slavery, repression was centralized and concentrated by capital. At the same time, this produced the collective laborer and a social process of work that developed a universal (although not undifferentiated) social worker. As capital concentrated the means of production and concentrated the proletarian class, the latter's rebellious nature grew. Monopoly capital becomes a "fetter on production" once the "centralization of the means of production and socialization of labor at last reach a point where they become incompatible" with their capitalist shell. That shell is "burst asunder. The knell of capitalist private property sounds. The expropriators are expropriated."[9]

He ends the chapter with a speculation on the relative violence of both revolutionary processes. The centralization and concentration of capital was "incomparably more protracted, violent and difficult than" would be the "transformation of capitalistic private property...

into socialized property."[10] The former entailed the dispossession, theft, and exploitation of the many by the few, while the latter might entail the expropriation of the few by the many.

After this revolutionary and succinct clarion call to expropriate the expropriators, Marx then turns to a relatively dull examination of Ebbon Wakefield's theory of colonialism in the final chapter, Chapter 33 — again moving from a mode of revolutionary presentation to inquiry. Marx appreciates Wakefield's theory for its honesty; Wakefield does not try to hide the violence of colonialism or exploitation through notions of equal and free rights, and he explicitly acknowledged the need for dispossession.

Marx ends Volume 1 by reminding us again that the capitalist mode of production and accumulation are based on expropriation, colonialism, genocide and slavery. He returns to the antagonistic class forces that animate Marxist theory and practice. The contradictions of capitalism that he has laid out — which cannot be solved within capitalism — do not necessarily lead to automatic revolution, if the contradictions can be displaced or managed through other forms of dispossession or super-oppression, such as colonialism. "Capital" Volume 1 ends then with an opening to further study and inquiry. If the revolutionary process in the prior chapter appeared predetermined and closed, the final demonstrates that there are no objective determinants guaranteeing victory outside of the class struggle.

MARX'S PEDAGOGIES IN ACTION

Marxist pedagogy is a never-ending alteration between inquiry and presentation, of trying to both understand the world and to explain the world to those social forces that must transform it. The key for Marx and for Marxist pedagogy is to keep these in tension, the need to both assert the answer (presentation) and to keep studying (inquiry). The emphasis will change depending on a host of circumstances.

In many fields of nonprofit organizing, there is a presentation that only an immediately realizable and "winnable" goal is valid, and therefore there is no space for inquiry and, more specifically, revolutionary inquiry. While revolutionaries fight for reforms in the here and now, we do not adopt reformism, which keeps us trapped within the present, unable to see beyond it.

As an alternative, revolutionaries link the fight for reforms to the end goal of the total revolutionary transformation and restructuring of society. This is not winnable by any one action, protest, campaign, etc., and so the end goal is there, but suspended; it is not self-evident how exactly it unfolds. When we organize with this ultimate goal in mind, it compels alongside our activism a process of continuous research and study. This, after all, is what drove Marx. Without the desire for a totally new world, we would not have Marxism.

The key point is that Marx left us not only distinct yet dialectically related educational processes; he also offered us examples of navigating between the two, as well as the various factors that shape which ones we engage. It is not that presentation or inquiry comes first or second, and it is not that one is good and the other bad. The communist organizer, leader, or teacher has to deploy both depending on different external and class or site-specific contingencies. Sometimes learning must take precedence, and studying must be suspended. At other times, studying must take precedence, we must be free to imagine alternatives, get lost in the possibilities, reach our dead ends, and open up inquiry to a new presentation and then to a new inquiry.

This might be what, in part, separates dogmatic Marxists from those who take it as a living, breathing document. The economists, for example, only learned Marx, while those who have made revolutions, like we will see clearly with the next chapter, have engaged Marxism as an infinite well of studying. □

Chapter 5
Liberator, theorist, and educator

Amílcar Cabral

BY CURRY MALOTT

A MÍLCAR Lopes da Costa Cabral was born September 12, 1924, in Bafatá, Guinea-Bissau, one of Portugal's African colonies. On January 20, 1973, at the young age of 48, Cabral was murdered by fascist Portuguese assassins just months before the national liberation movement in which he played a central role won the independence of Guinea-Bissau.

This particular struggle was waged for the liberation of not just one country — Guinea-Bissau, where the fighting took place — but also for another separate geographic region, the archipelago Cape Verde. Cabral and the other leaders of the movement understood that they were fighting in a larger anti-colonial struggle and global class war and, as such, their immediate enemies were not only the colonial governments of particular countries, but Portuguese colonialism in general. For 500 years, Portuguese colonialism was built upon the slave trade and the systematic pillaging of its African colonies: Mozambique, Guinea-Bissau, Sao Tome e Principe, Angola and Cape Verde.

Despite the worldwide focus on the struggle in Vietnam at the time, the inspiring dynamism of the campaign waged in Guinea-Bissau — together with the figure of Cabral — captured international attention. In the introduction to an early collection of Cabral's writings and speeches, Basil Davidson describes Cabral as someone who expressed a genuine "enduring interest in everyone and everything that came his way."[1]

Like so many revolutionary leaders Cabral was "loved as well as followed" because "he was big hearted" and "devoted to his peoples' progress." Due to his leadership and brilliance, "governments asked his advice" and "the United Nations gave him its platform."[2] However deserved it was, Cabral never indulged in this praise, and instead focused solely on his commitment to the liberation and self-determination of the world's working class and oppressed.

The Portuguese colonization of Guinea-Bissau was backed by Spain, South Africa, the United States and NATO. Summarizing the pooled imperialist power wielded by Portugal in a report on the status of their struggle Cabral elaborates:

> In the basic fields of economics, finance and arms, which determine and condition the real political and moral behavior of states, the Portuguese government is able to count more than ever on the effective aid of the NATO allies and others. Anyone familiar with the relations between Portugal and its allies, namely the USA, Federal Germany and other Western powers, can see that this assistance (economic, financial and in war material) is constantly increasing, in the most diverse forms, overt and covert. By skillfully playing on the contingencies of the cold war, in particular on the strategic importance of its own geographical position and that of the Azores islands, by granting military bases to the USA and Federal Germany, by flying high the false banner of the defense of Western and Christian civilization in Africa, and by further subjecting the natural resources of the colonies and the Portuguese economy itself to the big financial monopolies, the Portuguese government has managed to guarantee for as long as necessary the assistance which it receives from the Western powers and from its racist allies in Southern Africa.[3]

Despite the immense power of their enemies, the struggle led by the relatively small population in Guinea-Bissau prevailed, remaining a beacon of inspiration to this day.

As a result of his role as a national liberation movement leader for roughly 15 years, Cabral had become a widely influential theorist of decolonization and non-deterministic, creatively applied re-Africanization. World-renowned critical educator Paulo Freire, in a 1985 presentation about his experiences in liberated Guinea-Bissau as a sort of militant consultant, concludes that Cabral, along with Ché

Amílcar Cabral, center

Guevara, represent "two of the greatest expressions of the twentieth century."[4] Freire describes Cabral as "a very good Marxist, who undertook an African reading of Marx."[5] Cabral, for Freire, "fully lived the subjectivity of the struggle. For that reason, he theorized" as he led.[6]

Although not fully acknowledged in the field of education, Cabral's decolonial theory and practice also sharpened and influenced the trajectory of Freire's (1921-1997) thought. Through the revolutionary process led by Cabral, Guinea-Bissau became a world leader in decolonial forms of education, which moved Freire deeply.

That is, because of the villainous process of Portuguese colonialism, which included centuries of de-Africanization, re-Africanization, through decolonial forms of education, was a central feature of the anti-colonial struggle for self-determination.

CABRAL'S DIALECTICAL UNITY, BUILDING THE PARTY AND THE 'WEAPON OF THEORY'

Cabral engaged the world dialectically. As a theory of change, dialectics has been at the center of revolutionary thought since Marx and Engels. Cabral wielded it with precision. Dialectically grasping how competing social forces driving historical development are often hidden or mystified, Cabral excelled at uncovering them, and in the process, successfully mobilized the masses serving as the lever of change.

Cabral knew that the people must not only abstractly understand the interaction of forces behind the development of society, but they must forge an anti-colonial practice that concretely, collectively and creatively see themselves as one of those forces. To do so, however, the masses had to be organized into and represented by a Party.

Dialectically grasping how competing social forces driving historical development are often hidden or mystified, Cabral excelled at uncovering them, and in the process, successfully mobilized the masses serving as the lever of change.

In 1956, Cabral helped found the African Party for Independence, which later became The African Party for the Independence of Guinea and Cape Verde (PAIGC). The PAIGC was the first ever communist party in Guinea-Bissau and Cape Verde, and its founding was a monumental and inspiring feat.

In "The Weapon of Theory," a 1966 address in Havana, Cabral articulated the inseparability of national liberation and socialism, telling the attendees that "in our present historical situation — elimination of imperialism which uses every means to perpetuate its domination over our peoples, and consolidation of socialism throughout a large part of the world — there are only two possible paths for an independent nation: to return to imperialist domination (neo-colonialism, capitalism, state capitalism), or to take the way of socialism."[7]

Cabral had to build the party and its indispensable culture of militant discipline from the ground up. Cabral's ability to meet the new party members where they were as co-learners speaks to his role as a pedagogue of the revolution. Delivered as a series of nine lectures to PAIGC members in 1969, Cabral covers the basics of the revolution, including its organization. He describes the PAIGC as a party in the Leninist tradition by referring to it as "an instrument of struggle" comprised of those who "share a given idea, a given aim, on a given path."[8]

Of course, revolutionary crises do not emerge from the correctness of ideas alone, but are driven by deteriorating economic conditions, and a crisis in the legitimacy of the state and its ability to meet the peoples' needs. In the 1940s there were several droughts that left tens of thousands of Cape Verdeans dead. Portugal's barbarism and indifferent response, situated in the context of the mounting poverty and suffering within its African colonies, began to alienate even the most privileged strata of the colonial state.

What made Cabral one of history's great communist leaders, outside of the larger historical moment that provided an outlet for his talents, was his theoretically-informed tactical flexibility, which was essential for a constantly shifting balance of forces. In other words, in-the-midst-of-struggle decision making is enhanced by theory and organization, which enables the ability to quickly grasp the immediate and long-term implications of the shifting calculus of power.

For example, in 1957 in Paris, Cabral and two Angolans formed the Movimento Anti-Colonista of Africans from the Portuguese colonies during the Algerian War. The three, in Angola, would go on to form the Popular Movement for the Liberation of Angola. What developed was one of the toughest anti-colonial fights in Africa.

It is only fitting that in his opening remarks in the first of the nine 1969 presentations to party members Cabral would choose as his place of departure an explanation of PAIGC's "motto" or "theme," the phrase "unity and struggle."[9] Defining the concept of unity dialectically, Cabral insists that "whatever might be the existing differences" within the people, "we must be one, an entirety, to achieve a given aim. This means that in our principle, unity is taken in a dynamic sense, in motion."[10]

The idea that unity is a movement and process of composition means that it is "a means, not an end. We might have struggled a little for unity, but if we achieve it, that does not mean the struggle is over."[11] The Party's role here "is not necessary to unite the whole population to struggle in a country. Are we sure that all the population are united? No, a certain degree of unity is enough. Once we have reached it, then we can struggle."[12]

To explain struggle, Cabral likens it to the tension between centrifugal force and gravity. As a concrete example Cabral notes that for a spaceship to leave the Earth it must overcome the force of gravity. Cabral then characterizes Portuguese colonialism as an external force imposed upon the people and only through the combined force of the people united can the force of colonialism be overcome.

In the address, Cabral theorized the dialectical nature of movement and change focusing specifically on how the anti-imperialist struggle must emerge from the concrete conditions of each national liberation movement.

> We know that the development of a phenomenon in movement, whatever its external appearance, depends mainly on its internal characteristics. We also know that on the political level our own reality — however fine and attractive the reality of others may be — can only be transformed by detailed knowledge of it, by our own efforts, by our own sacrifices. It is useful to recall in this Triconti-nental gathering, so rich in experience and example, that however great the similarity between our various cases and however identical our enemies, national liberation and social revolution are not exportable commodities; they are, and increasingly so every day, the outcome of local and national elaboration, more or less influenced by external factors (be they favorable or unfavorable) but essentially determined and formed by the historical reality of each people, and carried to success by the overcoming or correct solution of the internal contradictions between the various categories characterizing this reality.[13]

Cabral knew that to defeat Portuguese colonialism in Guinea-Bissau, the liberation struggle could not merely reproduce the tactics of struggles from other contexts, like Cuba. Rather, every particular struggle has to base its tactics on an analysis of the specifics of its own context. For example, while acknowledging the value of the general principles Guevara outlined in his "Guerilla Warfare," Cabral commented that "nobody commits the error, in general, of blindly applying the experience of others to his own country. To determine the tactics for the struggle in our country, we had to take into account the geographical, historical, economic, and social conditions of our own country, both in Guinea and in Cabo [Cape] Verde."[14]

Responding to Guevara's argument, based on the experience of Cuba, that revolutionary struggles go through three predetermined phases or stages, Cabral stated:

In general, we have certain reservations about the systematization of phenomena. In reality the phenomena don't always develop in practice according to the established schemes. We greatly admire the scheme established by Che Guevara essentially on the basis of the struggle of the Cuban people and other experiences, and we are convinced that a profound analysis of that scheme can have a certain application to our struggle. However, we are not completely certain that, in fact, the scheme is absolutely adaptable to our conditions.[15]

Cabral's assessment was also informed by the dialectical insight that the conditions in any one country do not develop in a vacuum unaffected by external forces. Not only were deteriorating conditions in Portugal, the imperial mother country, shifting the balance of forces in favor of national liberation movements in its African colonies, but the emergence of these struggles coincided with the successful revolution in China in 1949.

Conscious of this larger dialectical totality — which points to the interconnection between seemingly separate, unrelated parts — Cabral consciously fostered solidarity with Portugal's working class. Representing the colonized Indigenous peoples of Guinea-Bissau Cabral successfully reached out to the oppressed of Portugal in solidarity against their common class enemy, the fascistic Portuguese capitalist/colonialist class.

With dialectical theory and the spirit of anti-colonialist and anti-capitalist unity the revolutionary forces in Guinea-Bissau routinely freed Portuguese prisoners of war.[16] Cabral used such occasions to make public statements designed to educate and win over Portugal's persecuted working class to shift the balance of power away from Portugal's fascist state.

Cabral spoke directly to the 20,000 Portuguese conscripts, urging them to consider their class interests above and beyond the national chauvinism their ruling class fed them:

In the framework of our struggle for national independence, peace and progress for our people in Guinea and the Cabo Verde Islands, the freeing of Portuguese soldiers captured by our armed forces was both necessary and predictable. This humanitarian gesture, whose political significance will escape nobody, is the corollary of a fundamental principle of our party and of our struggle. We are not fighting against the Portuguese people, against Portuguese individuals or families. Without ever confusing the Portuguese people with colonialism, we have had to take up arms to wipe out from our homeland the shameful domination of Portuguese colonialism.[17]

Central to this message, Cabral offered insights regarding the awful treatment of not only prisoners of war in Guinea-Bissau and Cape Verde, but of the civilian population as well:

Members of our armed forces captured by the colonial troops are generally given a summary execution. Others are tortured and forced to make declarations which the colonial authorities use in their propaganda. In their vain but nonetheless criminal attempt at genocide, the Portuguese colonialists carry out daily acts of terrorism against the peaceful inhabitants of our liberated areas, particularly against women, children and old people; they bomb and machine-gun our people, reducing our villages to ashes and destroying our crops, using bombs of every type, and in particular fragmentation bombs, napalm and white phosphor bombs.[18]

The liberation of the Portuguese was connected to the liberation of Portugal's African colonies. If the Portuguese ruling class began losing control in Africa, it could also fall in Portugal, and if it fell in Portugal, it would fall in Africa.

Rather than a theoretical position worked out abstractly in isolation, it was formulated practically. It had serious and determinant results. Portuguese officers refused orders to fight in Africa, and some formed an Armed Forces Movement that supported the demands for independence.

The Portuguese soldiers led a rebellion against fascism at home, which ended more than 40 years of fascist rule. It opened the door to a popular upsurge that nearly claimed power for the Portuguese workers. These social convulsions in the imperial center in turn facilitated the independence of Portugal's African colonies.

DE-AFRICANIZATION AND ANTI-COLONIAL RESISTANCE

The small region in West Africa that the Portuguese would claim as Guinea-Bissau contained more than a dozen distinct ethnic groups. Slavers worked tirelessly to sow divisions between them. These divisions enabled slavers to enlist one group to facilitate the enslavement of others. This anti-African divisiveness would lay the foundation for centuries of de-Africanization.

Describing the role of colonial education in this epistemic violence Walter Rodney, in his classic text, "How Europe Underdeveloped Africa," explains that, "the Portuguese...had always shown contempt for African language and religion."[19] Whereas secondary schools were established for colonists, education beyond two or three years of elementary school for Africans was rare. Consequently:

> Schools of kindergarten and primary level for Africans in Portuguese colonies were nothing but agencies for the spread of the Portuguese language...[T]he small amount of education given to Africans was based on eliminating the use of local languages.[20]

The devastation of such practices reflects reports that European colonists with smaller African colonial holdings like Portugal were amongst the most desperate and thus cruelest in their efforts at maintaining their occupations. Consequently, indigenous resistance to Portuguese colonialism was so widespread for so many centuries that colonial rule was always limited to specific regions. In other words, colonial forces were never completely able to conquer what amounts to the state power of indigeneity.

It is therefore not surprising that the Portuguese were not able to rely merely on state violence for social control, but required intensive ideological manipulation as well. The attempt to eradicate Indigenous languages and cultures was crucial. Toward these ends, the colonial authorities propagated a hypocritical discourse that claimed their colonies were integral to the metropolis or mainland while simultaneously brutally exploiting them.

PAIGC fighters with a Portuguese military
plane that had been downed, 1974.

FASCIST PORTUGAL AND THE STRUGGLE

The brutality in which the Portuguese ruling class managed its African colonies would eventually be directed at its own working class with a fascist turn in 1926. Rodney explains that "when the fascist dictatorship was inaugurated in Portugal in 1926, it drew inspiration from Portugal's colonial past."[21]

The decline of Portuguese capitalism that gave way to Portuguese fascism would only deteriorate with the global capitalist crisis of the 1930s. Consequently, the desperation of Portugal's capitalist class intensified. For example, when Salazar became the dictator of Portugal in 1932, he declared that the "new" Portuguese state would be built off of the exploitation of "inferior peoples."[22]

Whereas the French ruling class had moved to neocolonialism by 1960, Portugal's decline had rendered it still largely backward and feudalistic. Out of desperation, Portugal became even more dependent on ruthlessly exploiting peoples not just in its colonial holdings, but within its own national territory.

Fascist Portuguese leaders, therefore, employing increasingly violent forms of social control, rejected African demands for self-determination. In response to the growing wave of national liberation movements in their African colonies, the Portuguese establishment sent armed forces to repress the struggle. Rather than cower in the face of Portuguese fascism and overall deteriorating conditions, national liberation movements grew and spread.

RELATIONS WITH CHINA

Following the establishment of the PAIGC, Cabral settled in Guinea's capital, Conakry. Cabral immediately reached out to China's Guinean embassy in 1960.

Since the emergence of the People's Republic of China in 1949, China had established a clear commitment to the anti-colonial movements in Africa. For example, in 1955 at the Bandung Conference, in which 29 African countries participated, China established foreign policy principles based upon supporting oppressed nations' right to self-determination. In 1957, China organized the Afro-Asian Solidarity Conference and in 1960 founded the Chinese-African Peoples' Friendship Association, in which Cabral enthusiastically participated.

Cabral and other leaders of PAIGC became regular guests at the Chinese embassy in Conakry. In 1960, the PAIGC received an invitation from the Chinese Committee for Afro-Asian Solidarity to visit China. A delegation from the People's Movement for the Liberation of Angola (MPLA) was invited as well. During this visit, China agreed to use their military academies to train combatants from both the PAIGC and the MPLA.

Training included instruction in guerilla warfare, the history of the Chinese Revolution and agrarian revolution, and socialist theory. The first group trained in China would serve as the embryonic core of the PAIGC's fighting cadre.

As a result of Cabral's leadership and diplomacy, China would emerge as one of Guinea-Bissau's first supporters in the early stage of its struggle for independence. China provided the PAIGC with a great diversity of support, from weaponry to assistance broadcasting radio messages denouncing the regular, horrific crimes of the Portuguese military in Guinea-Bissau. With support from China on one hand, and

Portuguese brutality on the other, the anti-colonial struggle intensified between 1963 and 1974.

ANTI-COLONIALISM AND DECOLONIALITY

An important part of carrying out the national liberation movement entailed knowing what issues to organize around.

Based on his intimate understanding of the uniqueness of the agricultural situation in his country, Cabral knew that the primary economic issue the majority peasant population faced was not access to land, as was the case in other colonies. Rather, the issue was unsustainable trade deals that were particularly devastating given the colonial insistence on not farming for sustenance but for export through single-crop production.

The demand for cultural and political rights in the face of fascistic Portuguese colonialism was another demand that resonated widely. Cabral focused on the political developments required for building a united movement for national liberation. In his formulations, he argued that the armed struggle was intimately interconnected with the political struggle, which were both part of a larger cultural struggle.

Cabral's Marxist formulations on culture were important for the larger struggle and for resisting colonial education. He acknowledged that fascists and imperialists were well aware "of the value of culture as a factor of resistance to foreign domination," which provided a framework for understanding that subjugation can only be maintained "by the permanent and organized repression of the cultural life of the people."[23]

Resistance, for Cabral, is also a cultural expression. What this means is that "as long as part of that people can have a cultural life, foreign domination cannot be sure of its perpetuation."[24] In this situation then, "at a given moment, depending on internal and external factors...cultural resistance...may take on new (political, economic, and armed) forms, in order...to contest foreign domination."[25] In practice, the still living Indigenous cultures that led centuries of anti-colonial resistance would organically merge with, and emerge from within, the political and national liberation and socialist movements.

In practice, Cabral promoted the development of the cultural life of the people. Written as a directive to PAIGC cadre in 1965, Cabral encouraged not only a more intensified military effort against the Portuguese, but a more intensified educational effort in liberated areas of Guinea-Bissau. Again, while the national liberation/anti-colonial movement and the educational process of decolonizing knowledge are often falsely posed as distinct or even antagonistic, Cabral conceptualized them as dialectically interrelated:

> Create schools and spread education in all liberated areas. Select young people between 14 and 20, those who have at least completed their fourth year, for further training. Oppose without violence all prejudicial customs, the negative aspects of the beliefs and traditions of our people. Oblige every responsible and educated member of our Party to work daily for the improvement of their cultural formation.[26]

A central part of developing this revolutionary consciousness was the process of re-Africanization. This was not meant as a call to return to the past, but a way to reclaim self-determination and build a new future in the country.

> Oppose among the young, especially those over 20, the mania for leaving the country so as to study elsewhere, the blind ambition to acquire a degree, the complex of inferiority and the mistaken idea which leads to the belief that those who study or take courses will thereby become privileged in our country tomorrow.[27]

At the same time, Cabral opposed fostering ill will toward those who had studied or who desired to study abroad. Rather, Cabral encouraged a pedagogy of patience and understanding as the correct approach to winning people over and strengthening the movement.

This is one reason why Freire describes Cabral as one of those "leaders always with the people, teaching and learning mutually in the liberation struggle."[28] As a pedagogue of the revolution, for Freire, Cabral's "constant concern" was the "patient impatience with which he invariably gave himself to the political and ideological formation of militants."[29]

This commitment to the people's cultural development as part of the wider struggle for liberation informed his educational work in the liberated zones. Freire writes that it also informed "the tenderness he showed when, before going into battle, he visited the children in the little schools, sharing in their games and always having just the right word to say to them. He called them the 'flowers of our revolution.'"[30]

[Cabral's] commitment to the people's cultural development as part of the wider struggle for liberation informed his educational work in the liberated zones.

VICTORY BEFORE VICTORY

Even though Cabral was murdered before victory, the ultimate fate of Portuguese colonialism had already been sealed years before his death, and he knew it. For example, in a communique released on January 8, 1973, a mere 12 days before he was assassinated, Cabral concludes that the situation in Guinea-Bissau "since 1968... is comparable to that of an independent state."[31] Cabral reports that after dozens of international observers had visited Guinea-Bissau, including a United Nations Special Mission, the international legitimacy of their PAIGC-led struggle was mounting. It had become irrefutable that:

> Vast areas have been liberated from the colonial yoke and a new political, administrative, economic, social and cultural life is developing in these areas, while the patriotic forces, supported by the population, are fighting successfully against the colonialists to complete the liberation of the country.[32]

With this knowledge Cabral, again, denounces the "the criminal obstinacy of the Lisbon Government, which intensifies its genocidal colonial war against the legitimate rights of our people to self-determination, independence and progress."[33]

Making the case for the formation of a new internationally-recognized state, Cabral argues that the people of Guinea-Bissau, through the leadership of the PAIGC, were already functioning as such:

> While our people have for years now possessed political, administrative, judicial, military, social and cultural institutions — hence a state — and are free

and sovereign over more than two-thirds of the national territory, they do not have a juridical personality at the international level. Moreover the functioning of such institutions in the framework of the new life developing in the liberated areas demands a broader participation by the people, through their representatives, not only in the study and solution of the problems of the country and the struggle, but also in the effective control of the activities of the Party which leads them.[34]

To begin resolving this contradiction, in 1971 the Party voted to hold general elections in the liberated areas "for the constitution of the first People's National Assembly" in Guinea-Bissau. After eight months of debate, discussion and outreach, elections were successfully held in 1972 in all of the liberated zones.

Several months after the election, Cabral issued another statement referring to the creation of the People's National Assembly as "an epoch-making victory for the difficult but glorious struggle of our people for independence."[35] Underscoring how this was a collective achievement of unity and struggle Cabral offered his "warmest congratulations to our people."[36]

He reminded the people that "a national assembly, like any organ in any living body, must be able to function in order to justify its existence. For this reason, we have a greater task to fulfill in the framework of our struggle."[37]

Cabral then announced that the PAIGC would be calling its first National Assembly to formalize their constitution thereby proclaiming to the world they exist and are "irrevocably determined to march forward to independence without waiting for the consent of the Portuguese colonists."[38]

Yes, Cabral was killed before the final expulsion of Portuguese colonialism, but, in a very real sense, he still ushered in a new, independent state.

FREIRE AND CABRAL'S DECOLONIAL EDUCATION IN A LIBERATION GUINEA-BISSAU

As a pedagogue of the revolution Basil Davidson refers to Cabral as "a supreme educator in the widest sense of the word."[39]

The importance of education was elevated to new heights by Cabral and PAIGC leadership at every opportunity. It therefore made sense for the Commission on Education of the recently liberated Guinea-Bissau to invite the world's leading expert on decolonial approaches to education, Paulo Freire, to participate in further developing their system of education.

Freire was part of a team from the Institute for Cultural Action of the Department of Education within the World Council of Churches. Their task was to help uproot the colonial residue that remained as a result of generations of colonial education designed to de-Africanize the people. Just as the capitalist model of education will have to be replaced or severely remade, the colonial model of education had to be dismantled and rebuilt anew.

> The inherited colonial education had as one of its principal objectives the de-Africanization of nationals. It was discriminatory, mediocre, and based on verbalism. It could not contribute anything to national reconstruction because it was not constituted for this purpose.[40]

The colonial model of education was designed to foster a sense of inferiority in the youth. Colonial education, with predetermined outcomes, seeks to dominate learners by treating them as if they were passive objects, and thus forcefully represses the method of research or the logic of study at the expense of presentation and learning.

Part of this process was negating the history, culture and languages of the people. In the most cynical and wicked way, colonial schooling sent the message that the history of the colonized really only began "with the civilizing presence of the colonizers."[41]

In preparation for their visit Freire and his team studied Cabral's works and learned as much as possible about the context. Reflecting on some of what he had learned from Cabral, despite never having met him, Freire offers the following:

> In Cabral, I learned a great many things...[B]ut I learned one thing that is a necessity for the progressive educator and for the revolutionary educator. I make a distinction between the two: For me, a progressive educator

is one who works within the bourgeois classed society such as ours, and whose dream goes beyond just making schools better, which needs to be done. And goes beyond because what [they] dream of is the radical transformation of a bourgeois classed society into a socialist society. For me this is a progressive educator. Whereas a revolutionary educator, in my view, is one who already finds [themselves] situated at a much more advanced level both socially and historically within a society in process.[42]

For Freire, Cabral was certainly an advanced revolutionary educator. Rejecting predetermination and dogmatism, Freire's team did not construct lesson plans or programs before coming to Guinea-Bissau to be imposed upon the people.

Upon arrival Freire and his colleagues continued to listen and discuss learning from the people. Only by learning about the revolutionary government's educational work could they assess it and make recommendations. Decolonial guidance, that is, cannot be offered outside of the concrete reality of the people and their struggle. Such knowledge cannot be known or constructed without the active participation of the learners as a collective.

Freire was aware that the education that was being created could not be done "mechanically," but must be informed by "the plan for the society to be created."[43] Although Cabral had been assassinated, his writings and leadership had helped in the creation of a force with the political clarity needed to counter the resistance emerging from those who still carried the old ideology.

Through their process revolutionary leaders would encounter teachers "captured" by the old ideology who consciously worked to undermine the new decolonial practice. Others, however, also conscious that they are captured by the old ideology, nevertheless strive to free themselves of it. Cabral's work on the need for the middle class, including teachers, to commit class suicide, was instructive. The middle class had two choices: betray the revolution or commit class suicide. This choice remains true today, even in the United States.

The work for a reconstituted system of education had already been underway during the war in liberated zones. The post-independence challenge was to improve upon all that had been accomplished in areas that had been liberated before the war's end. In these liberated areas, Freire concluded, workers, organized through the Party, "had taken the matter of education into their own hands" and created, "a work school, closely linked to production and dedicated to the political education of the learners."[44]

Describing the education in the liberated zones, Freire says it "not only expressed the climate of solidarity induced by the struggle itself, but also deepened it. Incarnating the dramatic presence of the war, it both searched for the authentic past of the people and offered itself for their present."[45]

After the war the revolutionary government chose not to simply shut down the remaining colonial schools while a new system was being created. Rather, they "introduced...some fundamental reforms capable of accelerating...radical transformation."[46] For example, the curricula that were saturated in colonialist ideology were replaced. Students would therefore no longer learn history from the perspective of the colonizers. The history of the liberation struggle as told by the formerly colonized was a fundamental addition.

However, a revolutionary education is not satisfied with simply replacing the content to be passively consumed. Rather, learners must have an opportunity to critically reflect on their own thought process in relation to the new ideas. For Freire, this is the path through which the passive objects of colonial indoctrination begin to become active subjects of decoloniality.

Assessment here could not have been more significant. What was potentially at stake was the success of the revolution and the lives of millions. This is a lesson relevant to all revolutionaries who must continually assess their work, always striving for improvement. In this way it was clear to Freire that they must not express "uncontained euphoria in the face of good work nor negativity regarding...mistakes."

From their assessment then Freire and his team sought, "to see what was really happening under the limited material conditions we knew existed." The clear objective was therefore "to discover what could be done better under these conditions and, if this were not possible, to consider ways to improve the conditions themselves."[47]

What Freire and his team concluded was that "the learners and workers were engaged in an effort that was preponderantly creative"[48] despite the many challenges and limited material resources.

At the same time, they characterized "the most obvious errors" they observed as the result of "the impatience of some of the workers that led them to create the words instead of challenging the learners to do so for themselves."[49]

From the foundation Cabral played such a central role in building, and through this process of assessment, what was good in the schools was made better, and what was in error was corrected. As a pedagogue of the revolution Cabral "learned" with the people and "taught them in the revolutionary praxis."[50]

CONCLUSION

As we discussed in the second chapter, Freire's work and practice have inspired what has become a worldwide critical pedagogy movement, although this movement has in many ways abandoned its revolutionary foundations. Cabral is a centrally important, yet mostly unacknowledged, influence of this movement. The attention to decoloniality occupies one of critical education's most exciting and relatively recent cutting edges, which demands a more thorough return to Cabral and the revolutionary movements, figures and histories they animated.

Reflecting on Cabral's contributions to decolonial theory and practice a decade after his time in Guinea-Bissau, Freire, like Cabral before his death, continued to insist that, "we need to decolonize the mind because if we do not, our thinking will be in conflict with the new context evolving from the struggle for freedom."[51]

In the last prepared book before his death, subtitled Letters to Those who Dare Teach, Cabral's influence on Freire seems to have remained central, as he insisted that "it is important to fight against the colonial traditions we bring with us."[52]

As the socialist and anti-racist movement in the United States continues to grow in size and political sophistication, the educational lessons from the era of anti-colonial socialist struggles will also grow in relevance. □

Chapter 6

Dual power, base building and serving the people in the U.S. revolutionary movement

BY WALTER SMOLAREK

THE current period is the most favorable for socialists in the United States in decades. Against the backdrop of the Great Recession, waves of activity around the Occupy Movement, the Black Lives Matter movement and the Bernie Sanders campaign have produced a profound radicalization in political attitudes across society. Socialism is viewed favorably by close to half of the population and a substantial section of young people are sympathetic towards communism and Marxism.[1]

The key challenge facing revolutionaries in this moment is how to convert this explosion of pro-socialist consciousness into an organized force in society. While this includes the rapidly-expanding ranks of new cadres who are dedicating their lives to the cause of socialist revolution, a real organized force in society will draw its strength from the tens of millions of people who suffer the profound injustices of the capitalist system and are searching for an alternative. This base, or potential base, for the socialist movement can be found primarily amongst the 140 million poor people in this country.[2]

As communists and other radicals across the country grapple with this question, the concept of dual power has rightfully become a topic of considerable interest and debate. However, the working definition of dual power used by organizations and individuals is often so broad and general that it renders the term practically useless. As such, it is important to disentangle the concepts and history bound up in these discussions in order to think clearly about the way forward for those fighting for revolutionary change.

PROBLEMS WITH THE CONTEMPORARY DEBATE OVER DUAL POWER IN THE UNITED STATES

The bulk of the current debate over the role of dual power in a strategy for revolution in the United States rests on a relatively recent redefinition and decontextualization of the concept. It is effectively stripped of its meaning by becoming so broad that it could refer to almost anything. This, in turn, results in the misunderstanding and misapplication of tactics related to directly meeting the needs of the working class, building a base of support and ultimately making a revolution.

The Black Rose Anarchist Federation is among the more prominent organizations popularizing this new understanding of dual power. This reformulation of the concept has its roots in anarchist writings on the subject that emerged in the early 2000s, in the aftermath of the anti-globalization movement. As an expression of its current position, this organization republished an article last year called "Active Revolution," originally written in a 2002 issue of the publication The Northeastern Anarchist. It defines dual power this way:

> Dual power theorizes a distinct and oppositional relationship between the forces of the state/capitalism and the revolutionary forces of oppressed people. The two can never be peacefully reconciled. With the theory of dual power is a dual strategy of public resistance to oppression (counter-power) and building cooperative alternatives (counter-institutions). Public resistance to oppression encompasses all of the direct action and protest movements that fight authoritarianism, capitalism, racism, sexism, homophobia, and the other institutionalized oppressions. Building cooperative alternatives recreates the social and economic relationships of society to replace competitive with cooperative structures.[3]

It is hard to imagine what does not fall under such a broad definition. Instead of institutions like Venezuela's National Constituent Assembly or the Soviets of the Russian Revolution that have the capacity to exercise state power — to enforce the rule of either workers and the oppressed or the capitalist class — the "power" in dual power simply refers to the fact that there are two camps in society locked in conflict with one another; that the interests of the exploited and oppressed are opposite and irreconcilable with the interests of the exploiters and oppressors is no revelation. This is simply a restating of the materialist conception of history. That revolutionaries should participate in politics — the struggle for power in society — is a concept so elementary that it has little utility for those looking for a concrete strategy to pursue.

The actions prescribed by this particular approach to dual power are likewise impossibly broad. Two sets of activities are proposed: creating vehicles to wage direct struggle against the ruling class and carrying out direct services to meet the material needs of working people.

The first type of activity is referred to by Black Rose Anarchist Federation as action that "encompasses all of the direct action and protest movements that fight authoritarianism, capitalism, racism, sexism, homophobia and the other institutionalized oppressions."[4] This could be a group of employees organizing a union at their workplace or going on strike. This could mean a community campaign to hold a police officer guilty of brutality to legal accountability. It could also refer to residents in an apartment building holding a rent strike, students marching to demand free higher education or activists holding a sit-in to demand action on climate change. Of course revolutionaries should organize, but the question of strategy is to determine which of these struggles and tactics (and so many others) have particular social significance, under what circumstances they arise and gain that significance, and for which layers of the population.

The other side of the "dual power" approach encompasses essentially all other types of activities that could possibly be organized by revolutionaries, from community gardens and food drives to crowd-funding campaigns.

Beyond the extreme generality of the concept, there is an additional problem embedded in the popular understanding of the purpose of activities meant to "recreate the social and economic relationships of society to replace competitive with cooperative structures."[5] This recreates many of the errors that communists have long pointed out regarding the creation of worker cooperatives as a means of "overcoming" capitalism.

No enterprise, cooperative or capitalist produces all of the raw materials, machinery, software, means of transportation and other inputs necessary for its own functioning. These can only be acquired through commerce with other enterprises, which will rightfully understand efforts to overthrow capitalism as a threat to their own existence. Beyond the barriers of entry costs, scale and price competition in capitalism, if a cooperative is somehow able to carve out a spot for itself in the broader capitalist supply chain, would the capitalist state not make their activities illegal if they ever truly presented a threat to the rule of the capitalist class?

In addition, there is nothing inherently radicalizing about having one's needs met. There is a huge complex of nonprofit organizations funded by ruling-class foundation money — many of which mask themselves with radical-sounding language — that have been established in recent decades and that meet the needs of working people but in a political sense serve as a means to inhibit the development of revolutionary consciousness. Promoting direct service activities as a form of dual power undercuts the core of the revolutionary socialist program: to have a society where people's needs are met we need to expropriate the capitalist class, smash their state and establish a workers' state in its place.

DUAL POWER IN THE HISTORY OF SOCIALIST REVOLUTIONS

To think clearly about dual power, we have to put the concept in its historical and political contexts. Previous generations of revolutionaries have understood dual power as a highly unstable situation in society that lasts usually for a temporary historical moment. The revolution — the decisive seizure of state power by the working class and oppressed — resolves the question of dual power by shattering the authority of the old power and establishing the legitimacy of the new power. Alternatively, a counterrevolution restores the old power in a new form.

This concept originates in the Russian Revolution of 1917. In February, the year's first revolution took place, which overthrew the absolutist monarchy. In its place, a provisional government was set up that included representatives of the Russian capitalist class as well as the more moderate elements of the country's socialist movement. But this was not the only source of authority in society. Parallel to the provisional government, institutions called Soviets emerged representing the interests of the country's workers, peasants and rank-and-file soldiers.

Lenin labeled this peculiar situation "dual power," and elaborated on it in the pamphlet "The Tasks of the Proletariat in Our Revolution," written in the period after the February Revolution but before the socialist revolution in October:

> The main feature of our revolution, a feature that most imperatively demands thoughtful consideration, is the *dual power* which arose in the very first days after the triumph of the revolution.

> This dual power is evident in the existence of *two* governments: one is the main, the real, the actual government of the bourgeoisie, the "Provisional Government" of Lvov [the first Prime Minister of the provisional government] and Co., which holds in its hands all the organs of power; the other is a supplementary and parallel government, a "controlling" government in the shape of the Petrograd Soviet of Workers' and Soldiers' Deputies, which holds no organs of state power, but directly rests on the support of an obvious and indisputable majority of the people, on the armed workers and soldiers...[6]

> This remarkable feature, unparalleled in history in such a form, has led to the *interlocking of two* dictatorships: the dictatorship of the bourgeoisie (for the government of Lvov and Co. is a dictatorship, i.e., a power based not on the law, not on the previously expressed will of the people, but on seizure by force, accomplished by a definite class, namely, the bourgeoisie) and the dictatorship of the proletariat and the peasantry (the Soviet of Workers' and Soldiers' Deputies).

> There is not the slightest doubt that such an "interlocking" cannot last long. Two powers *cannot exist* in a state. One of them is bound to pass away; and the entire

Russian bourgeoisie is already trying its hardest everywhere and in every way to keep out and weaken the Soviets, to reduce them to naught, and to establish the undivided power of the bourgeoisie.

The dual power merely expresses a *transitional* phase in the revolution's development, when it has gone farther than the ordinary bourgeois-democratic revolution, *but has not yet reached* a "pure" dictatorship of the proletariat and the peasantry.[7]

A contemporary example of dual power can be found in Venezuela's Bolivarian Revolution. Parallel to the institutions of the bourgeois state — the presidency, the National Assembly, the Supreme Court, etc. — inherited by the revolutionaries after Hugo Chavez's 1998 election victory, there exists a "communal state" in formation. The basic units of the communal state are the communal councils, which were first formally created in 2006. Steve Ellner, a professor at Universidad de Oriente in Puerto La Cruz, Venezuela, explained in a 2009 article:

The community councils are horizontally structured, with all of their leaders (called *voceros*, or "spokespeople") working free of charge and considered of equal rank. Spokespeople can belong to no more than one of their council's various commissions, which include a communal bank, which handles grant money; a 'social controllership,' which monitors spending; and an 'employment commission,' which enlists qualified community members for remunerative jobs and attempts to ensure that they receive preferential hiring. All decisions, including the selection of spokespeople, are ratified in an 'assembly of citizens,' which represents the community council's 'maximum instance of decision making.'[8]

The communal councils are grouped together into federations called socialist communes, which carry out larger-scale projects and develop socially-owned productive industries called "communal enterprises." The framework for the communes is laid out in the 2010

Organic Law of Communes. Augusto Montiel, then a member of the National Assembly who now serves as Venezuela's ambassador to India, described the goal of the law at the time of its passage: "To put an end to the bourgeois state that we still have, we need to create conditions for the development of a community-based, communal, democratic, protagonistic and revolutionary state. That is, to create a state that doesn't allow power to be concentrated in the hands of a few privileged people."[9]

Dual power is highly volatile and involves constant clashes between the competing sources of authority.

While dual power today in Venezuela and in Russia in 1917 have their own unique characteristics, because of the particular historical circumstances they arose out of, there are fundamental common features. Both involve the creation of grassroots decision-making institutions based on the direct participation of the organized working class, which is capable of carrying out the functions of the state. Both emerged as the result of revolutionary situations that radically shifted power in society. As such, in both cases, dual power is highly volatile and involves constant clashes between the competing sources of authority. In Venezuela, this instability reached new heights in 2019 when the counter-revolutionary National Assembly backed Juan Guaidó's coup against President Nicolás Maduro, who had convened the National Constituent Assembly as the highest expression of revolutionary authority.

RELATED QUESTIONS ON BASE BUILDING

Direct services activities — what proponents of the new conceptualization of dual power refer to as "counter-institutions" — do indeed have a great deal of utility. However, the provision of direct service must be understood as a tactic, rather than a strategy in and of itself. Alongside the discussion in the socialist movement on the meaning and application of dual power, a related debate has emerged over base building.

For revolutionaries, base building refers to long-term efforts to create a durable reserve of support within a particular section of the working class. This is usually constructed on the basis of a workplace or a neighborhood. The provision of services is an important element

The North Front Street Community Block Party,
organized by the Philadelphia Liberation Center.

of base building work. But this needs to be done in a way that does not promote the view that the creation of a vast network of worker-owned cooperatives or activist-administered social programs is a path to power. Properly applied, "serve the people" programs are primarily an outreach tactic with the goal of identifying sites of potential class struggle, rather than a manifestation of dual power.

To consider some practical examples, the Philadelphia branch of the Party for Socialism and Liberation is involved in a number of base building activities that utilize direct service events along these lines. In May 2019, we organized a block party through our Kensington-based community center called the Philadelphia Liberation Center. At the block party, we distributed bags of household essentials and child care goods marked with our Party logo, and also organized music, childrens' activities and a cookout to give neighbors a chance to socialize. Events geared towards meeting residents' cultural and recreational needs can be just as effective as those aimed at meeting material needs, and has the added benefit of attracting in greater numbers the layers of the neighborhood with a baseline level of stability conducive to future organizing efforts.

Kensington is being intensely targeted by the big banks and real estate firms for gentrification. We made the right to housing the political theme of the block party, produced a special pamphlet for it, and promoted the event with the framing "strong communities can resist gentrification." In the course of our outreach for the block party, we met a long-time, well-respected resident of the neighborhood who was fighting the construction of a massive, luxury apartment complex on the small residential street where she lived. She invited us to attend an upcoming hearing on the construction, and from there to join the fight on an ongoing basis. The practical commitment to the well-being of people in the neighborhood demonstrated by the PSL's cadre earned the trust of the people, who invited us to intervene in this local issue. From there, we were able to help launch the Norris Square Community Action Network, which carried out a well-attended picket of the construction site and is also moving forward with other projects in the neighborhood.

Another practical example involves our work with a community of recently-arrived immigrants from Central America. Through a pre-existing contact, we were able to partner with a congregation to set up an after-school program called Escuelita Óscar Romero.[10] This project provides both child care and educational services to families struggling to survive under the weight of the U.S. government's war on immigrants.

Some time after Escuelita Óscar Romero was launched, the father of one of the participants was arrested by ICE and held for deportation. Because we had already developed a foundation of trust between ourselves and the people, we were able to immediately organize a well-attended meeting that resolved to form an anti-ICE emergency response network to prevent tragedies like this from happening again. We have subsequently held a number of door-knocking sessions along with members of the community to develop a contact list of people who are alerted when ICE is spotted in or around the neighborhood.

To build a base, communist cadre first need to insert themselves into the designated workplace or geographic location. Because this is a long-term effort, the reputation of the revolutionaries is of paramount importance. Working people will not follow any group into a struggle in sufficient numbers unless there is pre-existing trust and confidence that is established, and this is impossible to do through rhetoric alone. Direct service activities demonstrate, through practical deeds, that communists are upstanding members of the community who care deeply for the well-being of the people and sacrifice their time and resources for the benefit of others. Those most excited about these activities tend to be organic leaders in the community who are also the most receptive to struggle-oriented politics.

PREPARING FOR THE REVOLUTIONARY CRISIS

The pressing task of the day for those who seek a socialist transformation of society is not to build dual power, but rather to build a revolutionary party. The capitalist class is able to remain in power despite its microscopic size because it has at its disposal a state staffed by people who are effectively professional counterrevolutionaries dedicated to maintaining the status quo.

The only instrument that has historically proven capable of overcoming the entrenched power of the state is a revolutionary party composed of cadre — professional revolutionaries. But a revolutionary party cannot be constructed overnight. The ideological and practical training of its membership, the development of new generations of leadership and the recruitment of the most committed activists from a wide range of social movements is a long and painstaking process. Whether or not the revolutionary party has built deep, lasting bonds of trust and confidence with the workers and oppressed is of decisive importance.

Independent of the actions of the revolutionaries, a revolutionary crisis in society can and will occur. Usually brought about as a consequence of an economic crisis or a war, a revolutionary crisis is a brief period of time when the existing social order is so deeply despised and delegitimized in the eyes of the vast majority of the population that the state can no longer go on ruling in the old way. Under these circumstances, dual power in the true sense of the term can emerge, and the rule of the capitalists can give way to the rule of the people. □

Chapter 7

Pedagogy in the streets

Building organization and creating cadre

BY NINO BROWN

THE job of a revolutionary is to help make the revolution. In order to do this, we need to make more revolutionaries. Right now, our comrades are learning and struggling, all over the nation, on how to build mass organizations, how to strengthen and steel the party's ideological line, how to consolidate the gains our party has made, and how to build a revolutionary movement that is fundamentally anti-imperialist and anti-racist. More broadly, the masses are in motion everywhere. Capitalism is entering into another crisis period, although the objective movement of capital and its internal processes are beyond the scope of our control. What we do control are the subjective forces of the revolution: how organized, disciplined, ideologically steeled and connected we are to the masses of working and oppressed people.

THE PATH TO REVOLUTION IS ONE OF MANY OBSTACLES

As we have seen from the Egyptian revolution and the Occupy Wall Street movement of 2011, if we — the revolutionary forces who have a vision and program for the transformation of society — are weak or unable to strongly influence, if not lead the masses of people, then we will simply have a reconstitution of the same bourgeois social order with minor changes at best.

For the movement to grow into a force that can lend sustained leadership to the struggles of the masses of working and oppressed people, it is important that we assimilate the lessons from revolutionary movements that have not only challenged capitalism, but actually set out to build an alternative: socialism. As we are not academics, none of us are trying to wage a "war with words" and obscure the glaring necessity for fundamental social transformation. It is this necessity for socialism that drives all of what the party does. We want to be a vehicle for revolution — a body capable of holding together the various struggles of the masses of people and directing fatal blows to capitalism.

In "'Left-Wing' Communism: an Infantile Disorder," Lenin notes that "Russia achieved Marxism, the only correct revolutionary theory, through veritable *suffering*, through half a century of unprecedented torment and sacrifice, of unprecedented revolutionary heroism, incredible energy, devoted searching, study, practical trial, disappointment, verification and comparison with European experience."[1] We cannot state ahead of time that we can overcome every obstacle our class will face. We cannot even predict what obstacles will confront us. But what we can do is prepare ourselves by imbibing the lessons of not just Russia but of all the lessons of the global class struggle: from Egypt to France, from Venezuela to Nepal, and Greece to Turkey. We must learn from the suffering, sacrifices and victories of our comrades in struggle all over the world, for we are all linked by our common oppression under imperialism. If we refuse to learn, to assimilate and humble ourselves, we will certainly become obstacles to ourselves and to building a revolutionary movement.

MARCH WITH — NOT AHEAD OF — THE MASSES

Chinese revolutionary leader Mao Zedong describes two outlooks of revolutionaries who are "rightist" and "leftist" in their thinking:

> Those with a Rightist way of thinking make no distinction between ourselves and the enemy and take the enemy for our own people. They regard as friends the very persons whom the broad masses regard as enemies. Those with a 'Left' way of thinking magnify contradictions between ourselves and the enemy to such an extent that they take certain contradictions among the people for contradictions with the enemy and regard as counterrevolutionary persons who are actually not counterrevolutionaries.[2]

Today, we see various tendencies cropping up within the broad left and progressive movements. We have new forms of rightism and leftism, and while we must reflect on the past communist movements, this cannot substitute for an analysis of the concrete conditions of the day.

Some tendencies see no contradiction between building working-class power and collaborating with the Democrats. Oftentimes this comes up in our coalition and mass organization work where we run into individuals and organizations that cannot tell a friend from an enemy or an opportunist from a confused person trying to grapple with politics. At the same time, we run into those who are of the "leftist" orientation. They make enemies out of friends and obscure the contradictions among the people by magnifying our differences to the point where we are not only at each other's throats, but where our movement is unnecessarily circumscribed. These "leftists" march so far ahead of the people and magnify secondary and minor contradictions to the point where one would be left to believe that a revolution is not made by the masses of people but made solely by the reddest of red communists and socialists.

This is a grave error, which Assata Shakur affirms:

> ...without the support of the people, no movement for liberation can exist, no matter how correct its analysis of the situation is. That's why political work and organizing are so important. Unless you are addressing the issues people are concerned about and contributing positive direction, they'll never support you. The first thing the enemy tries to do is isolate revolutionaries from the masses of people, making us horrible and hideous monsters so that our people will hate us.[3]

No matter how "correct" our analyses are, if we fail to translate them into concrete policy, policies that not only "meet people where they are at" — which is often used as an excuse to keep people where they are at — and raise the consciousness of the masses,

After all, what does it mean for us that socialism is increasing in popularity? Does it mean that we simply declare loudly that we are socialists? Well, yes, but this is not enough, nor is it even primary for us. Even more important is that we demonstrate what is distinctive about our organization, which is that it is a vanguard party. Vanguard simply means to lead, and the party cannot declare itself as the van-

PHOTO: LIBERATION NEWS

Our cadres are to be shining examples of self-sacrifice and dedication. Our commitment to advancing the struggle to victory must be that of a 'professional revolutionary,' who carries on when others falter, or flee to safety and comfort.

guard — that must be left to the masses and history. As the Black Panthers put it, the vanguard is merely the tip of the spear, and the rest of the spear, the mantle or butt is what does the real deep damage. Our movement's ability to land blows against imperialism depend simultaneously on the sharpness of the vanguard and the determination of the masses. If the masses are determined and our links with them are deep and broad, then the spear will not only pierce our enemies but land a fatal blow.

REVOLUTIONARY THEORY AND THE 'PARALYSIS OF ANALYSIS'

Sometimes in our movement we see what Martin Luther King Jr. called the "paralysis of analysis," where activists and would-be revolutionaries are so caught in analyzing phenomena that they forget the essence of Marxism: the act of changing the world, not just understanding it.

In the work we do, we must have a mass-based approach. We cannot proceed from what we subjectively desire, but from a concrete analysis of the conditions. Many "leftists" make this error of subjectivism, of substituting their personal desire for what is necessary for a particular set of conditions.

No amount of revolutionary phrase mongering and flag waving can make a revolution. We have to merge theory and practice and make our politics speak to the people. Our comrades are activists and organizers. They are in the streets with the people, struggling in mass organizations to win demands of the masses, whether they be around housing and gentrification, prisons reforms, wages and union battles or the fight against police terror. Our campaigns, during this very polarizing time, seek to be a pole to draw all those disaffected by the system to socialist politics. We have a political program which puts forth demands as wide-ranging as reparations for African Americans, Hawaiians, and other oppressed nations; the dismantling of the U.S. imperialist state; and the combating of women's and LGBTQ oppression.

CADRES AND COMMUNICATIVE PEDAGOGY

It is not enough to simply join the Party. For us to truly develop a living and breathing body that can carry on the struggle in a highly concentrated way, after all the protests and street actions take place, we need cadre. The PSL has guidelines, a constitution and a program. These exist to help our members be disciplined. It is much harder to be disciplined now more than ever in the face of rampant individualism, facilitated by neoliberalism and amplified by social media.

An example of this is simple conduct online. At times, instead of trying to professionally and clearly explain things to people, we do what is sometimes referred to as "dunking" on people. This is where revolutionaries assume what is essentially an ultra-left position. We see ourselves as being "beyond" explaining things to people in terms they can understand. We forget that it is not what we say, but who is watching. And, who is watching (aside from the state!)? It is other working-class people! It is our friends, co-workers and other people in the movement. If we were to assume this position in real life, or "IRL" as people say today, we would isolate ourselves from the masses and the party would become irrelevant. We would be seen as standoffish and snobby, not the patient, disciplined and pedagogic comrades that we need.

Coming from bourgeois society, with all of its ills, we are inculcated with bourgeois individualism. We see our individual freedom as the endpoint and the axis of what we consider to be genuine freedom. Learning to take discipline from an organization (that isn't our job or boss!) and being expected to do more for the party, our mass organizations and ultimately the coming revolution, hurts our egos sometimes, but we outgrow that with the help of our cadres.[4]

Our cadres are to be shining examples of self-sacrifice and dedication. Our commitment to advancing the struggle to victory must be that of a "professional revolutionary," who carries on when others falter, or flee to safety and comfort. Our motto must be "for self nothing, for the masses everything!" Unlike the "leftists" who forget that they are a part of an organization and not a loose organization of like minded individuals, cadres know that a revolutionary vanguard is only as strong and solid as its members or cadre, who must be rooted among the masses in struggle.

It is vital that the cadre be good at communicating and connecting with oppressed people. We must be the natural leaders of the people whom others look to and seek the opinions of. If we use and abuse our social media and project ourselves simply as individuals, we fail to see that this will harm not only ourselves, but our organization. What good is having a program, guidelines and a constitution, if we simply continue to act as if we are just a social group or a group of like minded individuals?

Cadre must be patient, sensitive and tolerant, and most important, be good at listening. As a teacher I see the need for communication, patience, discipline, listening skills, collectivity, execution, going over mistakes, having a mind for the entire class and more, in order to move a body of people forward. Usually it is my classroom of 20 plus students, 9 to 11 years old, but the same applies to a revolutionary party.

As a teacher, my obligation is to teach all of my students, not just the most advanced or the most engaged. I have to listen to all of my students. I have to learn from all of my students. It is the same with being a revolutionary.

We must be serious, loving, disciplined, attentive, courageous, approachable, and most importantly, have a mass-based approach. If we simply parade around the most revolutionary of phrases, speak about revolution but not have a mind for the masses or the party, we will be muddleheaded phrase mongers caught in the "paralysis of analysis," isolated from the masses, and substituting fantasy for reality. □

Chapter 8

Militant journalism

The role of journalism in class society and in revolution

BY FRANK GONZÁLEZ AND GLORIA LA RIVA

Frank González is the director of Cuba's Prensa Latina news agency. This article is based on a December 2006 interview with Gloria La Riva. It provides background on Prensa Latina and the theoretical and practical considerations of revolutionary journalism, including the distinctions between "objectivity" and "impartiality," top-down and dialogical journalism, and bourgeois and socialist journalism.

FOR more than 47 years, Prensa Latina has been in the midst of all the important news developments that have taken place in Latin America and the rest of the world. In the 1970s and 1980s, it reached its greatest reach, with global coverage. We had 40 offices in an equal number of countries with information services in text, radio, television and photography.

At the start of the 1990s, Prensa Latina experienced a very difficult economic situation. We went through the disappearance of the socialist camp in Europe and the Soviet Union, with whom we had a special relationship of exchange and collaboration. We had to reduce our operation from 40 offices worldwide to 14 offices, all operating at a much-reduced level of personnel and with a lot of sacrifice. But the agency survived.

Our recovery began at the end of the 1990s. Today we have 23 offices abroad in addition to our headquarters in Havana. We have plans to expand by two offices per year.

Prensa Latina has a presence in Luanda, Angola, as well as in China and Vietnam. We are in Madrid, Moscow, Paris and Istanbul. And we have 16 offices in Latin America, practically in all parts of the continent. This year we will open in Kiev, Ukraine, where we will cover events in Moldova, Georgia and Poland.

Today, the flow of international information is in the hands of five large media conglomerates.

The agency transmits more than 400 daily dispatches and news stories in Spanish, English, Italian, Portuguese, Russian and, most recently, in Turkish. We have a strong presence on the Internet with 12 websites. This year we have had some 14 million visits to our sites.

About 50,000 media institutions and individuals in 147 countries receive Prensa Latina's news. Our multimedia division has produced more than 150 titles in CD-ROM, DVD and Super DVD formats.

We are currently moving towards the use of open-source software, specifically Linux, to operate within the Intranet, Extranet and Internet. The reach of our websites is constantly expanding.

'OBJECTIVE, BUT NOT IMPARTIAL'

The reasons that motivated the founding of Prensa Latina more than 47 years ago are more relevant today than ever.

Today, the flow of international information is in the hands of five large media conglomerates. If just 20 years ago there were 50 U.S. news organizations that controlled more than 90 percent of the international information flow, today there are only five. And of those five, four are U.S.-controlled and one is German. I say four from the United States because Fox, even though its owner, Murdoch, is Australian, is really a U.S. corporation. And those five media conglomerates do not only tell us what we should see, read or listen to. They tell us how we should see, read or listen.

Prensa Latina is more important than ever. We are very conscious of that. We journalists at Prensa Latina not only produce revolutionary journalism, but journalism of a very high quality. The bourgeois press presents itself as the defender of objectivity. The concept of objectivity arose in the 19th century as a feature of the U.S. elite's journalism. It was The New York Times that took the

PHOTO: PRENSA LATINA

Gloria La Riva (left) visits Prensa Latina. Havana, Cuba

lead in advancing the idea of objectivity as one of the attributes of supposedly independent journalism. [The use of objectivity by elite journalism (i.e. the corporate media) was advanced to hide or mask their capitalist-class bias.]

The concept of "objectivity" evolved in the 20th century not just as an attribute but as a standard. We also defend the concept of objectivity, but not just to defend it. We ourselves say that we are objective.

[Prensa Latina founder Jorge Ricardo] Masetti used to say, "We are objective, but not impartial." All discourse, including the media's discourse, implies intent. In terms of the media, it means an intent that is motivated by the relations of power, by market relations and by other such considerations.

Prensa Latina promotes a journalism that is different from that being produced today [by the media monopolies]. When we speak of alternative communication, we are not talking of just substituting one content for another. It is not simply a matter of journalism that is counterposed to the media monopolies. What we are talking about is creating a new form of journalism.

INTERACTIVE JOURNALISM AND
THE ROLE OF ALTERNATIVE MEDIA

The journalism of domination, of bourgeois journalism, is a top-down, unilogical and unidirectional journalism, in which an enlightened person becomes a transmitter issuing a message.

But we have reached a point where now everyone recognizes that the persons transmitting and receiving are constantly exchanging their roles in a communicative process, where both interact and enrich each other.

That is the journalism in which we place ourselves. When we speak of journalism that presents an alternative vision of reality, we are talking of a reality that is based on the truth.

It is the truth that José Martí spoke of, but it is also the truth that Bertolt Brecht spoke of. He said, "We have to search for the truth wherever it is, no matter how much they try to hide it. We have to convert the truth into a weapon, and to see in whose hands that truth is placed, so that truth reaches where it should."

For us, the alternative vision of reality is an anti-capitalist vision. What is the capitalist vision? The objective of capitalism is surplus value.

The system and the laws of the market create the institutions that make up capitalist society — the family, the church, the school, the youth and community associations and the means of mass communication.

All of this is meant to provide the system with the ideological support that prepares the citizens from birth to be raised and behave according to the laws of a system and the representation of reality that that system requires those citizens to have.

It would be naïve to think otherwise. The idea of an independent media and an objective press is a fantasy. I am not even referring to Marx in this case, but to Berger and Luckmann's "The Social Construction of Reality," to the sociologists who study knowledge, and to the philosophers and theorists of communication.

Therefore, each time that we in Prensa Latina witness the debate about "freedom of the press," "freedom of expression," "the independent press" and "objectivity," in reality these terms are being used in a discourse whose only aim is to conceal the class character of those institutions.

We do not have to conceal the class character of our journalism. What we do oppose and reject is the idea that there is a division between, on the one hand, professional journalism, and on the other, what is called militant or activist journalism.

We believe there is only one type of journalism and that we should defend journalism as a profession. We believe that just posting something on the Internet does not make one a journalist, although it is correct to say that the person who does so is carrying out an act of communication.

But the journalist has to have command of the narrative technique, command of the new technology of information and communication as a professional. Now, in this struggle to promote an alternative vision of reality, we believe that we cannot be exclusionary. That is why we call it an anti-capitalist vision. All those who are in favor of promoting a vision of reality that is polemical, that develops critical thought, that is a vision of totality, not totalitarian, that embraces all human thought in a general sense, we believe that all of us who believe in this should join together.

And we should make links, because there is something very important that can help us confront the enormous economic power and reach of the large media monopolies, and that is networking.

Information is circulated throughout all the interstices of the Internet. It allows us to establish alliances and exchange with each other, but in a flexible manner, where one does not direct or dominate others.

LATIN AMERICA AND THE MEDIA

The relation between the United States and Latin America is key. Latin America is emerging as a new pole of attraction. Latin American integration is on a course that is definitive and determined with the new processes taking place in the continental South. It is very important that the alternative U.S. press be aware of what is happening in Latin America and to see it from different angles to avoid stereotypes.

What the so-called "independent press" and "objective press" has tried to do throughout its history is to create stereotypes and make false claims.

For the "objective press," President Hugo Chávez is not a new Latin American revolutionary leader, inheritor of the best traditions of struggles of the peoples of our continent, but rather a putschist militarist who took power, who presides over a pool of petroleum, and who has a close relationship with Fidel Castro. And they present that relationship not as a great merit, as Chávez describes it, but as a stigma.

There is a very interesting alternative press in the United States that does good things and gives us the key to interpret what is happening in United States society. If you ask me as a journalist, I think that U.S. society is reaching the boiling point.

The political, economic and social conditions are being created that will cause that bubble to burst at some point. There we see what is happening in Iraq, what is happening in Afghanistan, what is happening in Latin America. The current United States administration insists on creating a false image of prosperity, a false image that the struggle against terrorism has to be fought thousands of miles away from the United States to "prevent them from coming here to attack us." It is based on the politics of fear and terror.

And within that U.S. society, where there are such noble and good people, we Cubans and Latin Americans have been able to experience solidarity and affection. We have seen it in concrete causes. If it were not for the solidarity of the people of the United States, Elián González would have not returned to his family as he did in June 2000.

It is the people of the United States who made it possible to stop the war in Vietnam. And it will be the people of the United States who will make it possible to stop the aggression and massacre of the Iraqi people.

A MODEL OF DIALOGUE

When we think of alternative communication we do not think of it as substituting one domination for another. It means establishing a model of dialogue that respects multicultural and multi-ethnic diversity, because the wealth of a society lies in its diversity.

In Prensa Latina, there is something we always need to clarify. The dialogue that we advocate is not with all members of society. We call for dialogue with those who are committed to an anti-capitalist vision. Dialogue with those who are committed to a capitalist vision is not dialogue. Such a "dialogue" will always be a struggle for power.

Although we say that the media is a tool of the system to consolidate the hegemony of the ruling class, it is not a simple process. It does not mean that behind each piece of information there is a conspiracy of a small group of millionaires who decide what to publish and how they will do it.

There are very complex processes that have a lot to do with the production routines of the media, that process of "newsmaking" that is so well researched in the United States, within which the hypotheses of "agenda-setting" and "framing" play their part.

INDEPENDENCE AND POWER

There is a generalized idea that the alternative media is an impoverished media, with few resources, not controlled by anyone, with no links to anything official. Let us talk about power. Jean-Jacque Rousseau, the French philosopher, wrote of the "natural person."

The baby, when it is born, is a natural person. But when it relates to its mother and begins to drink milk from the mother's breast, it becomes a social person. The baby has begun to interact with someone, and this creates a dependency on someone else. It is a dependency for food, the primary basic necessity for a human being.

But there also begins a relationship of power. The mother has a certain quota of power, that is, "I will feed you when I can feed you, or when I want to feed you." The baby cries and demands because it also exercises a quota of power, that is, "You have to feed me now." The baby becomes a social being.

Therefore, it is not possible to speak of the independence of even small media organizations, tiny ones that are very poor and lacking in resources. You will always depend on the orientation as to where you seek your power.

'JUST DOING MY JOB'

One of the things that capitalism tries to present to us, or to convince us of, is that historical processes do not count. Things are the way they are — simply because that is how it is.

Let us say I am part of U.S. society. For me the most important thing is myself and my family, and that is how it is because it has to be that way. The mentality in the United States says, "I do this no matter what happens because it is my job." Your job? How is it possible that Mrs. Madeleine Albright was the secretary of state of the United States, the sworn enemy of Cuba, and two weeks after leaving that post says the blockade of Cuba makes no sense?

Or Mr. Colin Powell, who stated recently in Dubai that there is a civil war in Iraq and that they committed an error with regard to Iraq. When he was the secretary of state he lied to the world, saying that there were weapons of mass destruction and that there were links between Iraq and al-Qaeda.

I was in New York City once, speaking with an executive of one of the large U.S. media chains. I asked him, "How can that happen?" He told me, "No, the problem is that they were doing their job."

IDEOLOGY AND EMANCIPATION

Yes, but what are the roots of that problem? It lies in the support for capitalism. I don't mean a capitalist who literally forces me to work with a whip. Rather, capitalism develops a mentality in the person that the most important thing is work.

But what [kind of] work? The part they pay me for my support? Of course, the capitalist converted my labor power into a commodity. And for that commodity to be better exploited, I need that mentality inculcated into my consciousness.

We believe that alternative communication has to give the person, the receiver, all the keys to be able to interpret the events. Everything that happens has a historicity, every event has an origin and a process of development. It is not like television, where images overwhelm us but, in the end, do not allow us to interpret events, and therefore, leave us with nothing. It is simply one of the tools that the bourgeois press uses to maintain its rule over the minds of people.

When we in Prensa Latina speak of alternative communication — again, we say alternative communication and not alternative journalism — in our opinion it means critical thought — anti-hegemonic, all-encompassing thought — a liberating and emancipatory thought.

I said earlier that the objective of capitalism is surplus value.

What is the objective of socialism? It is the emancipation of the human being. And we believe that alternative communication should act toward that goal of liberating humanity. □

Chapter 9

Interview with militant historian Sónia Vaz Borges

BY SÓNIA VAZ BORGES AND ANDIRA ALVES

This interview was originally published in the Spring 2021 issue of Breaking the Chains, *a one-of-its-kind feminist, socialist magazine, deeply connected to the everyday experiences of working women from generations past to today.*

Andira Alves: You mentioned being born in Portugal, child of Cape Verdean immigrants. How did you see our history being reflected in Portugal?

Sónia Vaz Borges: Well, if you look at the Portuguese school curriculum, we have a couple of moments and none of them are really uplifting. We have the so-called discoveries of when the Portuguese start to do their maritime travels around the world, then you have slavery and then you have colonization. Those are the three moments, at least in the history manuals. Normally you combine that with geography manuals regarding the African continent and images of war and starvation. None of it is really uplifting.

And when you go to history again and you talk about colonization and mention the colonial war, you have a small footnote about the liberation struggles. And you have maybe one or two pictures of Amílcar Cabral, Samora Machel, or Eduardo Mondlane. There's a small footnote and that's it. There's not really a connection and you don't see any reflection of that in the school manuals from what you learn and hear in conversations at home, conversations in the neighborhood, even the music reflects other aspects you don't see there.

Although Portuguese history is deeply intertwined with African history, it's only one side that is shown. The large African and African descendent community in Portugal does not see themselves reflected in official versions of Portuguese history. Then, of course, you have a clash in the classroom, in the school and in the playground because you do not see yourself represented.

And then if you add that to the initiatives to where these kids are invited to, the only invitations they receive are to dance or to cook. So if you compile all this information, then you see how disconnected the curriculum is and how the Portuguese mentality already sees the African community.

Andira Alves: I think that's especially interesting. My mom had all of her primary education in Cabo Verde, in Fogo. You still spoke only Portuguese and you were not able to speak your actual language, and what the repercussions of that are. Cabo Verde, being more isolated from the African continent, somehow became closer to Portugal. It does seem like a lot of Cape Verdeans do have that disconnect because of history and what they are taught. With that, what led to the African Party for the Independence of Guinea and Cape Verde (PAIGC) developing their militant education?

Sónia Vaz Borges: I think when we talk about PAIGC, which was founded in the 1950s, we have to look further back at the history of PAIGC. Otherwise, we place PAIGC in the middle of nothing. Before the PAIGC was actually founded, there were several other movements — movements in Portugal, Cape Verde, Guinea-Bissau, Angola, Mozambique and so on. PAIGC is a result of all these movements. For example, you have, in Cape Verde, the rebel[lion] of Ribeirão Manuel, then you have, in Guinea-Bissau, the rebel[lion] against the taxes that Africans had to pay. And then you have in Portugal, the centers like the African Study Center, which was a secret club where African students would join and talk about Africa, their situation in the metropolis and their situations in their lens [from their perspective]. If you put this all together, there's a long history, a long trajectory of the PAIGC.

To add to that, there were Pan-African movements happening during the 1920s in Portugal at that time. So the PAIGC comes as a result, one of the results of all these struggles. You cannot talk about the PAIGC without talking about Amílcar Cabral [who], with other comrades, founded the party in 1956.

And of course, then the party is created. The armed struggle starts, the program starts from a military civil[ian] radio, all these kinds of things that PAIGC created during the struggle. And of

Sónia Vaz Borges

course, you have the process of militant education, which you have to go further into the past of seeing, for example, the students' activities in Portugal, their own process of conscientization, which is part of militant education.

The militant education the PAIGC developed during the struggle is a reflection of what was already happening. Even for the party to exist, to be founded in 1956, it had to go through this process of education, of self-education, of self-decolonization. The PAIGC [emerges] as an extension of what was happening before [and what] was happening in a different situation because there was a situation of war, a situation of being a party that [had] its headquarters in a foreign country in Conakry, Guinea. It had to do with several other elements happening in the world like the Non-Aligned Movement, the anti-colonial movement that emerged with the Movimiento Anti Colonial, and in the 1960s it turned into the Conference of Nationalist Organizations of the Portuguese Colonies. You have all these combi-

Biography
(From Sónia Vaz Borges' Website)

Sónia Vaz Borges is a militant interdisciplinary historian and long-time social and political organizer. She was born and raised in Portugal by Cape Verdean immigrants who immigrated during the colonial period.

Vaz Borges holds a B.A. in Modern and Contemporary History-Politics and International Affairs from ISCTE-University Institute of Lisbon, and an M.A in African History from the Faculty of Humanities of the University of Lisbon and a Ph.D. in Education Sciences — History of Education from the Humboldt University of Berlin.

Her work includes editing "Cadernos Consciência e Resistência Negra" ("Notebooks Consciousness and Black Resistance"), "Na Pó di Spéra. Percursos nos Bairros da Estrada Militar, Santa Filomena e Encosta Nascente" ("In the Dust of Waiting. Paths in the neighborhoods of Estrada Militar, Santa Filomena and Encosta Nascente"), co-authoring the short film "Navigating the Pilot School" (2016); and "Militant Education, Liberation Struggle, Consciousness: The PAIGC education in Guinea-Bissau 1963-1978."

She currently works as a researcher at the Humboldt University Berlin, working on the project "Education for all" and a personal research project focused on The Walking Archives, the liberation struggle, memory, generation and imaginaries.

nations of small things, then you can see militant education not just as a school product but also as a long process of conscientization and decolonization at the same time.

Andira Alves: People have always been resisting and this did not come out of thin air. It was years of organization and trying different tactics and strategies before resulting in armed struggle. For women and young girls to have access to education became a priority task within the organization. What was the development of young girls and women like with the PAIGC?

Sónia Vaz Borges: Even within the PAIGC, you have highly educated women, which I find amazing. You have Dulce Almada Duarte who wrote her PhD thesis in Portugal. You have Ana Maria Cabral, the same thing. And then you go to Guinea-Bissau and you have a different group of women that are already politicized, but with no official degree. Then you go to the countryside and we have also, again, highly politicized women without knowing how to read and write, but highly politicized.

And what I found amazing in the struggle of the PAIGC is how these three groups just combine their forces. These three groups of women put their skills and their knowledge together to work toward their self-education or reeducation. Those who are studying in the Portuguese colonial schools, they still have to re-educate themselves in a decolonized way. And how do they put their skills and their strengths together to build themselves, to build this system or this organization that was the PAIGC? How do they place and conquer their space inside the organization?

That's why I call the liberation struggle an individual collective process response. Because it's not just [that] individual that turns into collective and collective that turns into individual. And it's not just, "it happens." It's a process and it's a response to something.

Andira Alves: Exactly. Going back to educational structures and things you take for granted like logistical planning for schooling. I saw pictures of teachers sitting on a log. How do you do this in the midst of armed warfare? What extra measures did schools have to take for students to attend?

Sónia Vaz Borges: I also had the same thought. What is my reference [to] schools? It's the reference that I know in Europe. Somehow your brain is so messed up, I'm referring to my brain, that you don't associate that it was an armed struggle in the forest, so of course, you cannot have the same infrastructure that I have as a reference.

In doing this work, this research forced me to deconstruct these ideas of the school as a building, of the need of having all this infrastructure, or how one can speak and think of an alternative infrastructure due to the conditions that they have at the moment.

It was to really take in consideration the situation of the country. You have two seasons in Guinea-Bissau: the dry season and the rainy season. You have to consider the time that people go to work in the fields. You have to take into consideration how much food is produced. You have to take into consideration where villages are located. All of this to determine where you can locate the school. You have to try to make sure that children can still go to school in a safe situation.

So the first PAIGC schools in the liberated zones were located in the barracks with the military because that was what was considered a safe space for children. But then they slowly started to realize that actually it was not a safe space because if the barrack was attacked, the kids were also attacked. They had to stop creating the schools in the barracks, but they can't put the school right close to the village because if the village is a target, the school would be a target.

So they have to build a school in a place in between. We have the boarding school in the North, and we have the boarding school in the South, but you don't have a specific location.

And then they also have to think about [having] water around, to build shelters, a bunker. So they have to build all these logistics around the school and then use the environment, the forest, as a protection against air raids, against even foot raids because it's still a guerrilla struggle.

They had to use all the knowledge that they had about the forest, which is more traditional knowledge or local knowledge and combine it with the guerilla knowledge in order to see where to put the school. And this is a combination of two kinds of knowledge that look so distant, but the PAIGC actually put it to work together for self-defense.

Andira Alves: The book — "Militant Education, Liberation Struggle, Consciousness: The PAIGC education in Guinea-Bissau 1963-1978" — discusses what is a militant educator. You could not separate your ideology from the school. They informed one another. School was during wartime. It was a teacher's responsibility to create a joyful ambience, both disciplined and attractive.

Sónia Vaz Borges: Teachers, they also have to have military training for defense of the school. And there were a couple of teachers who died from this duty of protecting the students.

There is also this idea of not teaching political education as something abstract. The situation, the conditions you are living [in] was already political education training.

So you cannot avoid to talk about the bombings. You cannot avoid talking about the exploitation. You cannot [avoid] talking about oppression. You feel that airplane flying over you and you're already like, "maybe I'll die today." You have to explain why there are airplanes flying around. So all these "whys" that are happening at the time of teaching is part of the political education. At the same time, the situation of war causes trauma in everyone.

So there is also this environment, and you can see [s]till today when you interview students and teachers, this love and care for each other that was central in the process of PAIGC political education. Militant education is not just a structure.

Andira Alves: You are now collecting these oral histories of adults and elders who were students during the liberation struggle. What was their reflection on their educational process or development during that time?

Sónia Vaz Borges: Well, none of them is a kid anymore. They're in their fifties [and] sixties. Their first reflection is, "if it wasn't the struggle, I won't be here in the position that I am, that I have today. I won't be a student. I won't know how to read and write. Probably, I would be working on the farm. I won't have the opportunity to study abroad, to become a lawyer, to become an architect, to become an engineer and to come and give my contribution to my country."

They say, "I am what I am today because of PAIGC. It doesn't matter how wrong the party went after independence, but I am what I am because of PAIGC. Because of the struggle that PAIGC initiated and the creation of the schools that gave me the opportunity to be what I am and have today." And that's their primary reflection. □

Appendix A

Formulating study and discussion questions

BY LIBERATION SCHOOL EDITORIAL COLLECTIVE

REVOLUTIONARIES study texts to understand and engage them from the perspective of our class and for the purpose of advancing the class struggle. What kind of questions do we face as revolutionaries? Having different kinds of questions enables us to probe and think about potentialities, possibilities and practicalities.

Broadly speaking, there are a few different kinds of questions that are helpful for learning, studying and discussing texts. Traditionally, they are presented as different levels of a "scaffold," in that only once you can answer one kind of question can you move onto the next. This kind of approach can be helpful, especially for facilitating discussion, because in order to apply and extend the ideas from a reading to our local and contemporary struggles, we have to first actually have a handle on what the ideas are. In a sense, the scaffolding approach can be useful because it ensures that we have a baseline understanding before we move to extending the ideas or synthesizing them.

At the same time, the scaffolding approach is based on the pedagogy of learning rather than studying, or, more precisely, it prioritizes learning over studying rather than dialectically engaging both. Learning facts, timelines, contexts, and so on, is incredibly important. But doing this alone, or always beginning here, implies a certain predetermined trajectory: that mastering facts and ideas must come before thinking about how to or how to process or apply such ideas. This is not always true; in the long process of studying, we are constantly accumulating knowledge and facts, reflecting on ideas, discussing them with others, combining them with our own experiences, and bouncing back and forth between all these mental processes in a way that is not strictly linear.

In view of this, the different kinds of questions we offer below are intended as a possible set of tactics you can deploy in formulating your own reading guides and collective discussions of texts. These tactics should be used flexibly and in relation to the overall goals of the outreach and educational program. The order of their presentation is not meant to be linear and we also try to include examples of questions from this book that can activate different forms of knowledge: comprehension, takeaways, identification of significance, analysis, synthesis and application. These examples and question types are not comprehensive, and readers can certainly think of their own in studying this book or others.

COMPREHENSION

The most straightforward kinds of questions are aimed at comprehending the content of the text. These are baseline questions that ensure we are understanding what the text actually says before we begin applying and extending it in our own contexts. Knowing a fact is one thing, but comprehension requires an understanding of how facts and ideas relate to make more complex ideas and concepts. Questions in this category can ask for readers to write more complicated ideas in their own words or to phrase them so that someone outside of or new to the struggle might understand.

You might include more comprehension questions for texts that are denser and more theoretical, or for texts that make references to other events, ideas, theorists or organizations readers might not be familiar with. For example, although Lenin is a very clear writer, his texts are primarily polemical. In order to get the essence of a text, it is not always necessary to know everything about the different trends of the movement he is engaging with. As a result, comprehension questions can help prevent the reader from getting lost in the weeds, so to speak.

- In Chapter 1, the author introduces Vygotsky's "Zone of Proximal Development." In your own words, write a one sentence definition of this concept; or draw a picture that represents the ZPD.
- In Chapter 2, what do you think the author means when they write that "We cannot divorce the methodology from the ideology, the theory from the method, or the critical from the pedagogy in Freire's work?"

- In Chapter 4, the author writes about the distinction between the method of inquiry and the method of presentation. How would you describe each method to someone new to the struggle? You can think generally or specifically (in terms of someone you are trying to recruit or bring into the movement's orbit).
- Chapter 6 argues that when revolutionaries perform direct service activities they are not creating "counter-institutions." Why is this the case?

TAKEAWAYS

These questions also promote comprehension, although they help participants understand the text from their own experiences. Personal takeaways generally ask readers and participants to focus on a broader set of themes and focus on what resonates with them the most.

- One of the sections in Chapter 5 is titled "Anti-colonialism and decoloniality." What one or two points stuck out to you the most and why?
- The beginning of Chapter 3 discusses bourgeois ideas of intelligence and socialist ideas. What is the most important distinction, and why?
- The socialist idea of intelligence is "broadly summarized." What specifics, if any, would you add to the socialist idea of intelligence, and why?
- Reflecting on your own experiences, have you ever been subjected to bourgeois standards of intelligence? Was this experience stifling, and, if so, how might socialist ideas of intelligence and forms of knowledge have helped you in this situation?
- What lessons from Chapter 7 can you take with you and your organization to better relate to and move the people?

IDENTIFICATION OF SIGNIFICANCE

These questions ask participants to think about why certain parts of the text are important. They can be combined with other kinds of questions, such as those aimed at comprehension.

- Chapter 8 makes a distinction between journalists being "objective" and "impartial." What is this distinction and why is it important for revolutionaries?
- Chapter 9 talks about the need to rethink schooling and education, and how this happened in the particular context of the PAIGC. What was most compelling to you about this process and why?
- Why do you think the qualities outlined at the end of Chapter 8 are so important for revolutionaries?
- Chapter 2 argues that Freire's dialogic pedagogy has to be seen as part of his political project, and says there is nothing inherently liberating about dialogic pedagogy. Can you think of examples of certain educational practices that are seen as inherently liberating but actually reinforce capitalist and other oppressive social relations?

ANALYSIS AND SYNTHESIS

Analysis and synthesis questions require us to critically examine and break down information into parts. We analyze motives, causes, and make inferences based on the evidence and information provided. By analyzing the parts of concepts or any given phenomena, analysis questions position us to have a better understanding of the whole. The whole may be a generalization or axiom, but is based on the concrete and meticulous analysis of component parts of a thing.

- What does the idea, in Chapter 2, that the teacher has to place the content of education in a particular context imply about the authority of the teacher?
- What other ways would you classify the distinctions between learning and studying from Chapter 4?
- What does the Zone of Proximal Development have to do with Freire's conception of dialogic pedagogy?

APPLICATION AND EXTENSION

Application and extension questions are the kinds that revolutionaries hunger after the most. These questions ask us to take something from the reading and either think of examples or use the idea to make sense of a contemporary issue or struggle. After all, the point of Marxism, of revolutionary theory, is not to simply interpret the world but to change it. Application questions require us to think as problem solvers who use the acquired knowledge, understanding and comprehension. This type of thinking and questioning require us to consider the facts, conditions, contradictions of various concepts and phenomena, as we approach solving problems. Revolutionaries fundamentally seek to change the capitalist social order and thus should center the testing of their theories and ideas in and through collective social practice.

- Chapters 1 and 2 focus on revolutionary educators who are well known in the United States but whose work has been divorced from its revolutionary context and importance. What other figures has this happened to? How can this provide an opening for moving people further to the left? What arguments or strategies would you use to try and accomplish this?
- Chapter 3 discusses fixed versus growth mindsets. What examples can you think of in your own experience where you or someone close to you has evidenced each kind of mindset?
- Have you ever had a fixed mindset approach to something? If so, what would have helped you change to a growth mindset?
- The end of Chapter 6 provides examples of "serve the people" programs that helped build support within communities and raise support for and trust in the Party's cadre. What — if any — are some direct service activities your organization could start that would help build a base amongst the local population? How would you plan to make these outreach programs create trust and solidarity with the population and build the Party? What long term goals would your organization have for these programs?
- Chapter 4 ends with an example of educational programs based solely on learning (presentation) and an example that combines learning (presentation) with inquiry (research, or studying). What other examples can you think of for each? How can these two dialectically-related pedagogies better inform your own organization's practices?

Appendix B

Teaching tactics

BY LIBERATION SCHOOL EDITORIAL COMMITTEE

THE following is a series of tactics you can use for teaching or facilitating an educational meeting. While we present them as distinct tactics, you can — and should — feel free to merge some together. Further, these tactics can be combined with the different study and discussion questions provided in the previous appendix.

INTRODUCTIONS

It is helpful to start an educational session with a brief round of introductions. There are an infinite variety of ways to do this. Especially if it is a group that does not know each other well, you can ask people to share their name, why they came to the event, how they heard about it, and what, if anything, they hope to get out of it. If it is an event for a specific organization, you might ask people to share why they joined the organization. If the group members know each other somewhat well, you can ask other questions to build community — anything from "what song is the soundtrack to your life right now" to "if you could live in any fictional setting from a movie, book, or television series, what would it be and why?" It is important to give people a minute to prepare their answers, and even more important to be strict about time, because introductions have a tendency to go longer than needed.

LECTURING AND PRESENTING

As we stated in the introduction, Marxist education presumes the competence of all involved. Relative to educational settings, this means that we should not assume that just because most of us are sitting silently watching one person speak that we are not active. In fact, listening and watching are active processes of engagement. There is an unfortunate trend in many progressive educational circles that devalues teaching and lecturing and sees it as inherently oppressive.

This can certainly be the case. Yet who watched the great — and long — speeches of the world's communist revolutionaries and asked if there could be time for worksheets or small-group work? How many people listen to podcasts, read articles, or watch news shows without also thinking and engaging in the content we are being exposed to? Who has not been moved to action by a rousing speech at a political demonstration? Who has not been won over to the cause, at least in part, because we finally heard someone explain the reasons for our poverty and oppression?

Delivering prepared speeches and presentations are important tactics in revolutionary education. In study groups, opening and closing with presentations can be especially helpful for providing participants with the historical, political, organizational and other context that is crucial to what we are studying but that we might not know. The important thing is that they are engaging and that they are not presented as the definitive and conclusive analysis that we all must uncritically accept. There might be times when presentations are the primary form of teaching that take place, with room for questions and answers at the end. There might be other times when they should be kept to a minimum, or where they are one tactic deployed among many.

FACILITATING DISCUSSIONS

Leading educational sessions by merely asking questions and responding to the first people to raise their hands can result in those who are the "fastest" thinkers or the most "confident" speakers to dominate the conversation. Especially under capitalism, this can reinforce existing hierarchies and forms of oppression such as racism and sexism. This is because many of our experiences in oppressive educational systems recognize certain groups as "knowledgeable" authorities (even if they are not).

Fortunately, there are a number of tactics you can use to include everyone who really wants to participate. Some of these involve individual reflection and writing, while others involve small group work or paired discussions.

THINK-PAIR-SHARE

This activity asks participants to think — and write — about a question for a period of time, usually between 3-5 minutes. For example, you could ask everyone to think about what they found to be the most relevant point in a reading and write about why and how they found it so relevant.

Then, participants are paired with another person to discuss what they wrote, usually between 3-10 minutes, depending on the prompt. You can pair them with whoever is next to them or, if space allows and you want the participants to get to know each other, you can move them around and have them count off and pair up that way. Sometimes, you might ask them to combine their definitions or writings into one, taking the best or more relevant parts from each.

Finally, the pairs go around the room and share what they have discussed. Often, participants organically identify connections between different pairs. The teacher could also write down the main points from each report back on the board, and use those points to facilitate a larger discussion.

It is important to tell participants the time limits for each part of this process ahead of time. This is especially true when it comes to the final sharing portion.

One reason to deploy this tactic is to facilitate participants getting to know each other. Another important reason is that often, after sharing their ideas with someone in a one-on-one setting, participants feel more comfortable and confident in sharing it with the entire group.

CONCEPT MAPS

This tactic asks participants to visually represent not only key concepts from the reading, but to trace links and connections between different concepts. For example, you might ask participants to identify the main idea from the introductory section of the text. Next, you ask them to think about how the idea is developed in the later sections of the text. Finally, you have students find a way to diagram the connections they have identified. This can take various forms — from Venn diagrams to flow charts.

QUOTE CURATION

For this activity, you isolate a certain section of the reading (if it is long) and give students time to find the one quote (or part of a quote) that they think is the most important. After, students can go around and share their quotes and why they found them significant. Alternatively, teachers or students can write them on the board and refer to the board for a large-group discussion. Another option would be to follow this activity with a presentation or lecture, in which case the teacher would reference the quotes on the board throughout their presentation.

JIGSAW PRESENTATIONS

These are usually small-group activities (anywhere between two to five people) where different groups take on different parts of a text to later present on. After breaking up into groups, the teacher assigns each group a section of the reading. Next, give all groups an appropriate time-frame (e.g., five, 10, 15 minutes) to revisit their portion, discuss it, and respond to any specific prompts you have assigned. For example, groups could be asked to come up with the three main points from their section, or they could be asked to write a two paragraph summary of it. Afterwards, each group has a certain amount of time to present to the rest of the group. The teacher can address any gaps or omissions from the presentations, or to help the different pieces of the jigsaw cohere.

MEDIA ANALYSIS

For this activity, the organizers come prepared with a relevant contemporary news article, song, video clip or other form of media. You could also bring in excerpts from other readings or articles about local struggles. Usually — but not necessarily — after engaging in a discussion about the content, students are asked to engage the media from the perspective of the text. The teacher can write and assign prompts such as: What would the author say about this? What would they add to it? What would they critique in it?

ROLE PLAY

Role playing activities can be developed in many different ways. For example, one approach is to ask participants to practice elevator speeches by simulating an outreach situation where one person plays the role of the organizer and the other person the community member of workers being reached out to. In some situations the teacher can prepare scripts for participants to practice with each other before practicing without the scripts. In other situations the teacher may ask participants to generate their own scripts.

Another example of role playing may be less focused on preparing to launch a specific campaign and more about engaging with a specific text or historical event. In these instances the teacher may need to make more elaborate preparations. For example, a text outlining a complex constellation of class forces and their development over time might provide an opportunity to write scripts, roles, interests, etc. for all actors assigning specific characters or entities to individual participants accompanied with directions to facilitate their engagement with each other and comprehension and ultimate application of the material. □

Endnotes

Introduction: Revolutionary education and the promotion of socialist consciousness

1 Brian Becker, "Theory and Revolution: Addressing the Break in Ideological Continuity," *Liberation School*, accessed Oct. 27, 2021, www.liberationschool.org/theory-and-revolution-addressing-the-break-of-ideological-continuity/.

2 Karl Marx and Friedrich Engels, "Marx and Engels to August Bebel, Wilhelm Liebknecht, Wilhelm Bracke and Others (Circular Letter)," trans. P. Ross & B. Ross, in *"Marx and Engels Collected Works,"* vol. 45 (New York: International Publishers, 1991), 408.

Chapter 1: Vygotsky and the Marxist approach to education

1 Vygotsky's work is particularly significant for challenging decontextualized and racialized conceptions of mind because there is a tendency in capitalist schooling to attribute students' actual level of development with innate or biological factors, thereby ignoring the ways unequal and highly segregated educational systems produce unequal outcomes.

2 V.I. Lenin, "First All-Russia Congress on Adult Education: Speech of Greeting," in *Learning with Lenin: Selected Works on Education and Revolution*, ed. D.R. Ford and C.S. Malott (Charlotte: Information Age Publishing, 1919/2019), 24.

3 James Wertsch, *Vygotsky and the Social Formation of Mind* (Cambridge: Harvard University Press, 1985), 10.

4 Lev Vygotsky, *Mind in Society: The Development of Higher Psychological Processes* (Cambridge: Harvard University Press, 1978), 86.

5 Ibid.

Chapter 2: Paulo Freire and revolutionary leadership

1   Paulo Freire, *Pedagogy of the Oppressed* (New York: Continuum, 1970/2011), 54.
2   Ibid., 58.
3   Ibid., 80.
4   Ibid.
5   Peter McLaren, *Life in Schools: An Introduction to Critical Pedagogy in the Foundations of Education*, 6th ed. (Boulder: Paradigm Publishers, 2015), 241.
6   Freire, "Pedagogy of the Oppressed", 125-126.
7   Ibid., 126.
8   Ibid.
9   Ibid., 134.
10 V.I. Lenin, "What is to be Done?" in *Essential Works of Lenin*, ed. H.M. Christman (New York: Dover Publications, 1902/1987), 67.
11 Ibid., 156.
12 Freire, *Pedagogy of the Oppressed*, 138.
13 Lenin, *What is to be Done?*, 137. For more on Lenin's pedagogical theory, see Derek R. Ford, "Joining the Party: Critical Education and the Question of Organization," *Critical Education* 7, no. 15 (2016): 1-18.
14 Tyson E. Lewis, "Mapping the Constellation of Educational Marxism(s)," *Educational Philosophy and Theory* 44, no. S1 (2012): 98-114.
15 Freire, *Pedagogy of the Oppressed*, 183.
16 Ibid.

Chapter 3: Comrades: Made, not born

1   Kathleen M. Cain and Carol S. Dweck, "The Relation Between Motivational Patterns and Achievement Cognitions Through the Elementary School Years," *Merrill-Palmer Quarterly* 41, no. 1 (1995): 25-52.
2   See Angela Duckworth, *Grit: The Power of Passion and Perseverance* (New York: Scribner, 2016) and Privanka B. Carr and Claude M. Steele, "Stereotype Threat and Inflexible Perseverance in Problem Solving," *Journal of Experimental Social Psychology* 45, no. 4 (2009): 853-859.
3   Kenneth J. Saltman, "The Austerity School: Grit, Character, and

the Privatization of Public Education," *symploke* 22, nos. 1-2 (2014): 41-57.

4   Melissa Dahl, "Don't Believe the Hype About Grit, Pleads the Scientist Behind the Concept," *The Cut*, accessed Oct. 27, 2021. https://www.thecut.com/2016/05/dont-believe-the-hype-about-grit-pleads-the-scientist-behind-the-concept.html.

Chapter 4: Research and presentation

1   Karl Marx, *Capital: A Critique of Political Economy (Vol. 1)*: A Critical Analysis of Capitalist Production, trans. S. Moore & E. Aveling (New York: International Publishers, 1867/1967), 28.

2   Eric J. Hobsbawm, "Introduction," in *Karl Marx, Pre-Capitalist Economic Foundations*, ed. E.J. Hobsbawm, trans. J. Cohen (New York: International Publishers, 1964), 10.

3   Louis Althusser, *Lenin and Philosophy and Other Essays*, trans. B. Brewster (New York: Monthly Review Press, 1971), 70.

4   Antonio Negri, *Marx beyond Marx: Lessons on the Grundrisse*, trans. H. Cleaver, M. Ryan, & M. Viano (Brooklyn: Autonomedia, 1991), 9; 12. Negri was a leading theoretician and organizer of the "autonomous" school that participated in the Italian Civil War in the 1960s-70s before being falsely arrested in 1979 for kidnapping the former Italian Prime Minister Aldo Moro of the Christian Democratic Party. He was later exonerated, but was still facing 30 years in prison. Yet in 1983, he was elected to Parliament and used parliamentary immunity to escape to France to continue researching and organizing. He only returned to Italy in 1997 to serve out his remaining (and bargained-down) 13 years to raise awareness of the political prisoners still being held behind bars. While in prison, he co-wrote the (in)famous book *Empire* with Michael Hardt.

5   Karl Marx and Friedrich Engels, "The Manifesto of the Communist Party," in *The Marx-Engels Reader*, 2nd. ed., ed. R.C. Tucker (New York: W.W. Norton, 1978), 476.

6   Marx, *Capital*, 225.

7   Ibid., 262 f2.

8   Ibid., 714.

9   Ibid., 715.

10 Ibid.

Chapter 5: Amílcar Cabral

1   Basil Davidson, "Introduction," in A. Cabral, *Unity and Struggle: Speeches and Writings of Amílcar Cabral*, trans. M. Wolfers (New York: Monthly Review, 1979), x.
2   Ibid., xi.
3   Amílcar Cabral, "The Development of the Struggle." Accessed Oct. 27, 2021, https://www.marxists.org/subject/africa/cabral/1968/tds.htm.
4   Paulo Freire, "South African Freedom Fighter Amílcar Cabral: Pedagogue of the Revolution," in *Critical Pedagogy in Uncertain Times: Hope and Possibility*, ed. S. Macrine (New York: Palgrave, 2020), 171.
5   Ibid., 178.
6   Ibid., 179.
7   Amílcar Cabral, "Weapon of Theory: Address delivered to the First Tricontinental Conference of the Peoples of Asia, Africa and Latin America Held in Havana in January 1966." Accessed Oct. 27, 2021, https://www.marxists.org/subject/africa/cabral/1966/weapon-theory.htm.
8   Cabral, *Unity and Struggle*, 85.
9   Ibid., 28.
10 Ibid., 28-29.
11 Ibid., 31.
12 Ibid., 31.
13 Ibid., 32.
14 Amílcar Cabral, "Practical Problems and Tactics," 1968. Accessed Oct. 27, 2021, https://www.marxists.org/subject/africa/cabral/1968/ppt.htm.
15 Ibid.
16 Amílcar Cabral,"On Freeing Portuguese Soldiers," 1968. Accessed Oct. 27, 2021, https://www.marxists.org/subject/africa/cabral/1968/ofcpsI.htm.
17 Ibid.
18 Ibid.
19 Walter Rodney, *How Europe Underdeveloped Africa* (New York: Verso, 1972/2018), 304.
20 Ibid.

21 Ibid., 244.
22 Ibid.
23 Cabral, *Unity and Struggle*, 139.
24 Ibid.,140.
25 Ibid.
26 Amílcar Cabral, "Tell no Lies, Claim no Easy Victories," 1965. Accessed Oct. 27, 2021, https://www.marxists.org/subject/africa/cabral/1965/tnlcnev.htm.
27 Ibid.
28 Paulo Freire, *Pedagogy in Process: The Letters to Guinea-Bissau* (New York: Continuum, 1978), 18.
29 Ibid., 19.
30 Ibid.
31 Cabral, *Unity and Struggle*, 277.
32 Ibid.
33 Ibid.
34 Ibid., 278.
35 Ibid., 288.
36 Ibid., 289.
37 Ibid.
38 Ibid.
39 Davidson, "Introduction," x.
40 Freire, *Pedagogy in Process*, 13.
41 Ibid., 14.
42 Freire, "South African Freedom Fighter Amílcar Cabral," 170.
43 Freire, *Pedagogy in Process*, 14.
44 Ibid., 17.
45 Ibid.
46 Ibid., 20.
47 Ibid.
48 Ibid., 28.
49 Ibid.
50 Ibid., 33.
51 Paulo Freire, *The Politics of Education: Culture, Power and Liberation*. (London: Bergin & Garvey, 1985), 187.
52 Paulo Freire, *Teachers as Cultural Workers: Letters to Those who Dare to Teach* (Boulder, CO: Westview, 1977), 64.

Chapter 6: Dual power, base building, and serving the people in the U.S. revolutionary movement

1 Mohamed Younis, "Four in 10 Americans Embrace Some Form of Socialism," *Gallup*, 10 May 2019. Accessed Oct. 27, 2021, https://news.gallup.com/poll/257639/four-americans-embrace-form-socialism.aspx.

2 Poor People's Campaign: A National Call for Moral Revival, "Our Demands." Accessed Oct. 27, 2021, https://www.poorpeoplescampaign.org/about/our-demands.

3 Adam Weaver, "Active Revolution: Organizing, Base Building, and Dual Power," *Black Rose Anarchist Federation*, 29 March 2019. Accessed Oct. 27, 2021, https://blackrosefed.org/base-building-dual-power/.

4 Ibid.

5 Ibid.

6 V.I. Lenin, "The Tasks of the Proletariat in our Revolution (Draft Platform for the Proletarian Party)," in *Lenin Collected Works (Vol. 24): April-June 1917*, trans. B. Isaacs (Moscow: Progress Publishers, 1917/1980), 60.

7 Ibid., 60-61, emphasis in original.

8 Steve Ellner, "A New Model with Rough Edges: Venezuela's Community Councils," *Venezuela Analysis*, 11 June 2009. Accessed Oct. 27, 2021, https://venezuelanalysis.com/analysis/4512.

9 Ibid.

10 Felipe Neri, "Escualita Óscar Romero in Philadelphia Builds Unity in the Face of Anti-Immigrant Terror," *Liberation News*, 23 August 2019. Accessed Oct. 27, 2021, https://www.liberationnews.org/escuelita-oscar-romero-in-philadelphia-builds-unity-in-the-face-of-anti-immigrant-terror.

Chapter 7: Building organization and creating cadre

1 V.I. Lenin, *"Left-Wing" Communism: An Infantile Disorder* (Peking: Foreign Language Press, 1920/1975), 8, emphasis in original.

2 Mao Zedong, *Quotations from Chairman Mao Zedong* (Peking: Foreign Language Press, 1972), 49.

3 Assata Shakur, *Assata: An Autobiography* (New York: Lawrence & Hill, 1987/2001), 181.

4 Ben Becker, "Social Media and Democratic Centralism: Opportunities

and Challenges." *Liberation School*, accessed October 20, 2021, https://liberationschool.org/social-media-and-democratic-central-ism-opportunities-and-challenges/